The Sea

HAS NO END

Copy-Editor: Lloyd Davis
Design: Andrew Roberts
Printer: Transcontinental

Library and Archives Canada Cataloguing in Publication

Suthren, Victor, 1942-
    The sea has no end : the life of Louis-Antoine de
Bougainville / Victor Suthren.

Includes bibliographical references.
ISBN 1-55002-519-8

    1. Bougainville, Louis Antoine de, comte, 1729-1811. 2. Explorers—France—Biography. 3. Soldiers—France—Biography. 4. Sailors—France—Biography. 5. Canada—History—Seven Years' War, 1755-1763—Biography. 6. United States—History—French and Indian War, 1755-1763—Biography. 7. France—Biography. I. Title.

G256.B6S87 2004   944'.034'092   C2004-904462-1

1 2 3 4 5   08 07 06 05 04

  Canada

We acknowledge the support of the **Canada Council for the Arts** and the **Ontario Arts Council** for our publishing program. We also acknowledge the financial support of the **Government of Canada** through the **Book Publishing Industry Development Program** and **The Association for the Export of Canadian Books**, and the **Government of Ontario** through the **Ontario Book Publishers Tax Credit** program, and the **Ontario Media Development Corporation's Ontario Book Initiative**.

Care has been taken to trace the ownership of copyright material used in this book. The author and the publisher welcome any information enabling them to rectify any references or credit in subsequent editions.

J. Kirk Howard, President

Printed and bound in Canada
Printed on recycled paper

www.dundurn.com

Dundurn Press	Gazelle Book Services Limited	Dundurn Press
8 Market Street	White Cross Mills	2250 Military Road
Suite 200	Hightown, Lancaster, England	Tonawanda NY
Toronto, Ontario, Canada	LA1 4X5	U.S.A. 14150
M5E 1M6		

The Sea Has No End

THE LIFE OF LOUIS-ANTOINE DE BOUGAINVILLE

BY VICTOR SUTHREN

THE DUNDURN GROUP
TORONTO

In memory of
David M. Stewart

Table of Contents

Introduction

Louis-Antoine de Bougainville was an extraordinarily able French military and naval officer whose life encompassed many of the significant events in eighteenth-century Western history and who led a remarkable career that took him from the boudoirs of Paris to the flintlock battlefields of North America and on to the lush islands of the South Pacific. Gifted and urbane, thoughtful and articulate, he was a highly civilized observer of the terrors of the Seven Years' War in Canada and the flawed administration of New France that fought a losing battle against the overpowering English forces of Prime Minister William Pitt. After the war and the French loss of Canada, Bougainville expended much of his personal fortune trying to establish destitute Acadians in a settlement on the Falkland Islands, and when that successful effort was thwarted by politics, he turned his energies to a voyage of Pacific exploration and world circumnavigation that rivalled the first voyage of the Englishman James Cook both in its daring and its concern for the health of seamen. From that voyage Bougainville produced an account of the apparent paradise of Tahiti that landed like a bombshell on a jaded and static European society fascinated by the neoprimitive social concepts of Jean-Jacques Rousseau and the Encyclopedist movement in France. To a degree not yet fully explored, Bougainville's account contributed to the ferment of discontent within the vastly unfair European society of the eighteenth century that led in 1789 to the outbreak of the French

Revolution. Bougainville contributed personally to another great revolutionary upheaval, the American War of Independence, when he commanded the van of the French fleet off Yorktown that prevented the Royal Navy from relieving the encircled British army of Lord Cornwallis. The victory off Yorktown, for which Bougainville received much of the credit, marked the end of British hopes of suppressing the rebellion, and a peace treaty establishing the United States of America followed soon thereafter.

As the storm cloud of the French Revolution broke over France, Bougainville, due to the popularity he had enjoyed from his crews as well as his non-aristocratic background, managed to bridge for a while the enormous social divide between the elites and the people. For a brief time he held senior command in the Revolutionary navy, only to relinquish it when the general social turmoil made any command structure unworkable. At the height of the Terror, his reputation did not prevent him from being imprisoned, but the death of Robespierre led to his release. Napoleon respected Bougainville, and in the course of time Bougainville was named a Senator and Count of the Empire, dying amidst great honour and general admiration in 1811.

Beyond his abilities as a soldier and commander, however, Bougainville displayed intellectual skills and an omnivorous fascination with the natural world that made him every inch the Enlightenment man. Mathematical ability allowed him to write a treatise on integral calculus that won him a fellowship in Britain's Royal Society at a time when the two nations were at war, and the journals of his experiences in North America and the Pacific were full of observations on his environment, both social and natural, that drew on a knowledge of Greek and Latin scholarship. Fluent in English, a capacity that made him the negotiator of terms with his British adversaries on more than one occasion — including the surrender of Montreal in 1760 that effectively ended the Seven Years' War in North America — Bougainville was in many respects the international citizen which was the ideal of the educated eighteenth-century gentleman; loyal to his Crown and nation as honour demanded, but a member of a civil and literate fraternity which knew no political boundaries. In his life are visible both the limitations and the most admirable principles of the eighteenth-century world, and his significance as a player in some of the most momentous events in history, and as a mirror of those events, is remarkable.

Yet there was more than bewigged formality to Bougainville; true to the nature of his time, he embraced its sensual appetites with equal gusto as he did its intellectual delicacies. Not tall, and given to a certain stockiness, he revelled in the thundering gallop of a hunter across fields or over hedgerows, and became a superb swordsman through hours of ferocious swordplay. A fine shot with pistol, musket or fowling piece, he chafed at the inactivity of the lawyer's life his father had wanted for him, and embraced instead the action and movement of the military life. Gifted with a charming personality and an optimistic warmth, he restrained himself very little in the enjoyment of society, and particularly the world of women, where he was welcomed for his intelligent humour and considerate gallantry as much as for his evident ardour. That women found him a delight both in the salon and in the intimacies of the boudoir was evident in the long list of women with whom his name was associated, ranging from ingénue Parisian actresses to Iroquois village girls, and perhaps to Madame de Pompadour herself. A more revealing testament to his nature is the fondness and friendship with which these lovers viewed him, long after the relationships had ended.

In Bougainville's life we are able to see not only his varied and remarkable achievements but also the tumultuous panorama of the age that gave birth to the nations of North America, changed the kingdoms of Europe forever in a tidal wave of revolution and war, and introduced into Western thought the myth, if not the reality, of an earthly paradise. We are able to see how the articulate and sensitive courtier was changed into a somewhat dismayed warrior by the savage forest warfare of Canada, and how that experience affected the impact of Tahiti on him, and the subsequent effect of his observations there upon Europe. And finally, we are able to follow an appealing, articulate adventurer in his personal role in the actions and events that have shaped our own history. Like his

English contemporary, James Cook, Bougainville's life ultimately cast a longer shadow than could have been predicted at its beginning. Like Cook's, it was a life deeply affected by the experience of Canada. And, like Cook's, it was a life of courage and daring, of determination and imagination, yet also one of appealing humanity and warmth.

This book examines Louis-Antoine de Bougainville's early life and career, from his birth in Paris to his rejection of a law career and his enlistment in the army. It will examine the social connections and service that saw him sent to London as part of a diplomatic mission, and his subsequent posting to Canada as aide-de-camp to the French military commander there, the Marquis de Montcalm. It will then look at the wider context of the Seven Years' War, and will then use Bougainville's own journal to follow the events of the struggle and Bougainville's participation in its clashes and forest warfare alongside Indian warrior allies. Particular emphasis will be placed on Bougainville's perceptive observations on the nature and character of the Indian nations he encountered during his service in Canada. After examining the capitulation of Canada and Bougainville's role in negotiating the terms, the book pays particular attention to Bougainville's experience of Tahiti and his written impressions of its society. The impact of those impressions on Europe, and the reaction which occurred due to the writings of Bougainville and Cook will be examined, in particular the myth or reality of the seeming discovery of a terrestrial paradise. The book will examine Bougainville's naval career during the American Revolution, including his key role in the naval action off Yorktown in 1781, and the controversy that surrounded his actions in the French naval defeat off the Saints in 1782. Lastly, it will examine his experiences during the French Revolution, his brush with death at the time of Robespierre, and his final days of recognition and honour under Napoleon.

I am indebted to the Archives Nationales and the Bibliothèque Nationale, Paris, for access to material relating to Bougainville; to M. Pascal Geneste of the Service Historique de la Marine, and M. Jean-Marcel Humbert of the Musée de la Marine, Paris, for similar assistance; to the National Archives of Canada, Ottawa; and to the libraries of the University of Ottawa, Carleton University, McGill University, and Fort Ticonderoga, New York. A particular thanks is extended to the library of the Stewart Museum at the Fort, Montreal, where Eileen Meillon was of invaluable and patient help. I am grateful to Kirk Howard and the Dundurn Group for their kind patience awaiting this book, and Westwood Creative Artists for their encouragement and advice. I must also thank my wife Lindsay for her perceptive criticism, and my editor at Dundurn Press, Lloyd Davis, for his meticulous and wise editing.

It is my hope that a popular retelling of this remarkable man's life may provide not only a greater understanding of the eighteenth century, when so much of the modern world's foundations were laid, but an appreciation of the gifts that both French and British men and women of conviction and ability brought to the creation of the nation-states of North America, and particularly to Canada, which draws to this day on the wellspring of their combined achievements.

Victor Suthren
Ottawa, Ontario

Chapter One
Beginnings and Early Career

On the morning of November 12, 1729, the small but elegant home at 21, rue de la Barre du Bec in Paris was the scene for the arrival into the world of a healthy baby boy whose birth, though into fortunate circumstances, gave little hint that he would be present for the fall of a vast French empire in North America, circumnavigate the globe, be instrumental in the launching of the American Republic, and write imagery that would help shatter the society into which he was born. As Pierre-Yves de Bougainville, a notary at the Chatelet, or Paris courts of law, was allowed by the midwives to embrace his wife, Marie-Françoise, they held only the hope that the small, squalling bundle in her arms would survive the dreadful infant mortality of the age. Soon christened Louis-Antoine, the newcomer, it was hoped, might measure up to the already bright promise of a seven-year-old elder brother, Jean-Pierre, and two other children.

The Bougainville family had arrived in Paris some years earlier from Picardy — although it is unclear when — possibly from the village of Bougainville, which lies near Amiens. In previous years there had been Sieurs de Bougainville, but Pierre-Yves no longer had claim to the escutcheons of familial aristocracy, even though as a member of the Paris justiciary he was technically part of the *noblesse du robe*. The status of nobility in eighteenth-century France could be achieved by a variety of means far more complex than the relatively simple basis of inheritance or royal favour which held in Britain. By the mid 1700s, France had some 16,000 traditional aristocrats and an additional 80,000 individuals who claimed nobility achieved by a wide variety of means. The great landowning families of ancient lineage were the *noblesse d'épée*, or *noblesse de race*, to whose ranks members could be added on the basis of letters patent from the king or the appointment of an individual to a fiefdom or office which required nobility. Military service, by mid century, led to ennoblement when the rank of general was obtained, but efforts of bourgeoisie to achieve nobility by the expedient of purchasing a military commission were blocked by the eventual demand of the traditional nobility that army commissions be given only to their sons — a prejudice which may have contributed to Louis-Antoine's pursuit of an eventual naval career rather than a military one. Holding high municipal office could lead to membership in the *noblesse de cloche*, and Louis-Antoine's father, Pierre-Yves de Bougainville, qualified for the numerous ranks of the *noblesse de robe*, whose members formed the legal profession. They sat as members of the numerous and ill-defined *parlements* that were a precursor to the revolutionary assemblies of 1789. But noble status could, in the final analysis, still be simply purchased, as with the *noblesse des îles*, formed of merchants who had made fortunes in the slave and sugar trades. It was a vast and complex system of status, title and position, membership in which ambitious Frenchmen sought if only because it excused them from paying any tax and set them apart from their neighbours: two facets of division and national weakness that would contribute to the collapse of the social structure under the hammer of the French Revolution.[1]

Within this complex web of hierarchy and privilege, Pierre-Yves had followed in a family tradition of a career in the law, as both his father and grandfather had, and he had every expectation that some, if not all, his male children would follow in his footsteps. His own dutiful attentions to his career led to his becoming, in later life, an *echevin* or council member for the city of Paris. That he had married well proved no hindrance to a respectable career as a member of the Parisian *haute bourgeoisie*.

His wife, born Marie-Françoise d'Arboulin, was a bright and vivacious young woman whose family was of some distinction, and whose connections and relations were to prove of great use to the young Louis-Antoine. In particular, her brother Jean Potentin d'Arboulin, who served in numerous government posts including that of *directeur des postes de l'Orléanais* — a position of grand title, if obscure duties — would become a confidante and close friend of the king's mistress, Madame de Pompadour. *La Pompadour* came to call d'Arboulin "Bou-bou," and his abilities, combined with her support, led him to the post of *secrétaire du cabinet du roi* in the service of Louis XV. As Louis-Antoine grew into manhood, d'Arboulin became a protector, a mentor, and finally a friend who provided not only guidance and advice to his nephew, but also invested money in Louis-Antoine's activities such as the Acadian settlement on the Falkland Islands. In a parallel to the career of Louis-Antoine's contemporary, James Cook, Louis-Antoine thus secured in his life the support, encouragement and assistance of a key patron whose efforts did much to advance his career. It was a pattern to be repeated throughout his lifetime, wherein something in his character, his abilities or his nature regularly brought forward someone to help him and encourage him. That the eighteenth century was an age of such "interest" as being key to social success was a given. But there was more to the support given Bougainville, something that suggests his combined powers of charm, competence and a simple likeability were beyond the usual. His friends and admirers would range from Madame de Pompadour to the emperor, and from Huron warriors to common seamen. It was an indication of the nature of Bougainville's character that he managed these relationships in a manner that earned him enduring respect from all whom he knew, of whatever station in life: a remarkable epitaph in its own right.

The young family to which Louis-Antoine was now the fourth addition consisted of the eldest, Jean-Pierre, born in 1722; Marie-Françoise, born in 1727, and who would marry Louis-Honorat de Baraudin, the governor of the small Loire Valley town of Loches;

and a third child who did not survive infancy. Louis-Antoine, arriving in 1729, was to be the last of Marie-Françoise d'Arboulin's children, as she died when Louis-Antoine was five years old. It was a bitter blow to the little boy, who remembered its pain all his life.

For Pierre-Yves de Bougainville, the challenge of raising three young children and pursuing his notarial career now loomed, and he turned anxiously to his family for help. It came in the form of his sister Charlotte, who arrived to take over the governance of the children. From what can be learned, Charlotte was a demanding presence who offered very little of the comfort and love Marie-Françoise had given her children, and Louis-Antoine suffered under the double hurt of his mother's loss and the imposition of this iron rule. It is tempting to speculate that these circumstances may have given Louis-Antoine a lifelong attraction to women and an unending search for their approbation and the refuge their arms afforded. There was nothing of the cad about him, nor a relentless Casanovan harvesting of female affection; nonetheless his need for their "society" was a constant in his life, and may have caused one of the two most controversial occurrences in his career, as will be later examined. Meanwhile, the little boy found the motherly care and affection he craved in the household of immediate neighbours on the Rue de la Barre du Bec, that of the Hérault de Séchelles family. Louis-Antoine had become a playmate and inseparable friend to a boy of the family his own age: Jean-Baptiste Hérault de Séchelles. As Aunt Charlotte tightened her steely grip on the family, Louis-Antoine found himself more and more at the Hérault home, and gradually the warm and welcoming Madame Hérault de Séchelles became a surrogate mother to the little lad, one he would address all his life as *chère maman*. With this de facto entry into her family, Louis-Antoine also entered into her formidable sphere of influence, which was to become a defining force as he grew toward adulthood.

Chère maman was, properly, Catherine Hérault de Séchelles, the daughter of Moreau de Séchelles, who had been *contrôleur générale des finances* to the royal court after having served as an *intendant*, or senior administrative officer, in the French army. His name was to be lent to islands taken by France in the Indian Ocean in 1756 — misspelled as the Seychelles — and when Catherine married René Hérault, the *lieutenant générale de police* of Paris, her children, including Jean-Baptiste, were ennobled by the status of *noble de ventre*. Into this well-connected household in Paris, and to their country home and its estate at Beaumont-sur-Oise, Louis-Antoine won access. Fortune had taken away a beloved mother from the little boy, but had given him not only the value of a "good" birth in a highly stratified and exclusive society, but a relationship with a family and a woman who gave him priceless advantage within it. It did not take long for Louis-Antoine's young plant to thrive in such nourishing soil.[2]

Louis-Antoine's brother, Jean-Pierre, was seven years his senior and a somewhat aesthetic youth who suffered badly from asthma. He followed dutifully in his father's footsteps, receiving his education at the Collège de Beauvais and becoming a lawyer as well as a brilliant classical scholar. In addition, he had a fascination with geography and chart-making, and his younger brother was immersed in an atmosphere of inquiry, learning, and fascination with the nature of the world. Jean-Pierre's abilities led to his appointment as assistant to Nicolas Freret, a cartographer and secretary of *l'Académie des Inscriptions* in 1745, and election to the *Académie française* in 1746 for his work in the classics. In 1749, on the death of Freret, Jean-Pierre was appointed to the post. He was thus in a position to aid and support his younger brother's career and development, although his own was hampered by the asthma that would eventually lead to his early death. In contrast to the openness his brother would display, Jean-Pierre also was governed by a traditional, somewhat narrow philosophy that accepted little of the optimism and universalism of the Enlightenment then emerging in European intellectual society.

Pedant though he might have been, Jean-Pierre's interest in the science of cartography may have planted in the young Louis-Antoine an interest in the wider world beyond Europe, which would bear fruit in the Pacific voyage to come, and may have

THE SEA HAS NO END

been the burr under the young man's career saddle that made him restless rather than comforted by the security of a Parisian lawyer's life; certainly Jean-Pierre did all he could to encourage the skills and abilities he saw emerging in his stocky, robust younger brother, having the youth at his elbow as he edited and published Freret's hand-drawn collection of more than a thousand maps and charts.

Louis-Antoine was at first sent into a similar educational path as Jean-Pierre, based on a rigorous immersion in the classics, and it had been intended that he, too, would wear lawyer's robes. The portents, at first, were good: Louis-Antoine was intelligent and diligent and he mastered Latin. Virgil became his favourite author, and throughout his life he would make liberal use of classical allusions and quotations, frequently from the *Aeneid*. It was also evident that he had a bent for mathematics, and when Louis-Antoine was nineteen, Jean-Pierre arranged for him to become a student of an honoured mathematician and astronomer, Alexis Clairaut, who lived not far from the Bougainville home. Clairaut also had an abiding interest in geography, and had taken part in an expedition to Lapland to measure the flattening of the earth at its poles. Louis-Antoine also soon became a pupil of another mathematician, Jean le Rond d'Alembert, who was part of the group of scholars under Diderot who authored the *Encyclopédie*. As the geographical historian John Robson has pointed out, it was the conjunction of the influences of these two extraordinary mathematical minds upon that of the young Louis-Antoine that was to transform him within two years from a competent mathematician to an excellent one. Bougainville — and here we can begin to distinguish him thus — was soon able to write a synthesis and clarification of integral calculus, entitled simply *Traité de calcul intégrale,* which, after presentation to the *Académie des Sciences* in 1753, appeared in print in two volumes, one in 1753 and the other in 1756. The work so impressed the Royal Society in London that it awarded membership to the young Bougainville in 1756, notwithstanding the state of war that existed between France and Britain.[3]

As he approached his twentieth birthday, an image of Louis-Antoine de Bougainville becomes more distinct. He is a stocky, physically strong youth, troubled somewhat by the same asthma that would kill his brother. He is intelligent, versed in the classics, literate, and a superb mathematician; he is a student at the University of Paris for whom a future of legal robes, brilliant conversation in the intellectual salons and the dignity of membership in the *nobles de robe* in the world's most prized urban community seemed assured. There is no key yet to his personal character, his charm or his social graces. The world he has lived in has ensured instruction in the effortless elegance and refined manners of a gentleman, mandatory in the pursuit of success in the salon — no crudity of any stripe admissible there. At this stage in his life, Bougainville could have stayed with the legal profession, developed further as a deskbound thinker as Clairaut and d'Alembert had done, and gradually been woven into the fabric of the Parisian intellectual community, marrying well, remaining secure in the web of family connection and influence and becoming an elegant footnote in the story of European thought and civility. Instead, Bougainville completed his legal studies, and was duly admitted to the bar, only to set it all aside. To the complete surprise of his family and his *saloniste* colleagues, he announced that he would become a career soldier.

There had been a parallel influence at work in his life to the intellectual and mathematical one, and it was best seen in his friendship with Jean-Baptiste Hérault de Séchelles. It was with this boyhood companion that Bougainville had expressed a vigorous masculinity that was somewhat at odds with the powdered delicacy of the salon, even though the ideal of the age called for ease in both worlds. Bougainville was not tall, but his sturdy form revealed a surprising strength and athletic ability, and with Jean-Baptiste, Bougainville roamed the Hérault de Séchelles country estate, revelling in physical effort and adventure. He became a crack shot with pistol and flintlock fowling piece, and an accomplished horseman, thundering off with Jean-Baptiste at full gallop in the laneways, fields and forests of Beaumont-sur-Oise. With a third friend, Chailly, Bougainville and Jean-Baptiste took instruction in swordplay and would practise until exhausted for hours daily, indoors and out, until Bougainville became lethally expert with the gentleman's weapon.

And there was romantic gallantry as well: while not yet twenty, Bougainville was known to have had an intimate relationship with a striking young actress, known as *la Clairon* — and others were reputed. At the age of twenty-one, even before his decision to take up the career of a soldier, Bougainville had anchored all this libertine energy with the socially wise step of enlisting, along with Jean-Baptiste, in the *mousquetaires noirs*. This largely ceremonial regiment, part of Louis XV's "household" troops, was a training ground for aspiring young officer candidates hoping to catch royal or other courtly favour and "interest." Bougainville was aware of the continuing tensions with Britain over issues that remained unresolved after the War of 1739–1748, but a clear commitment to the military had not yet arisen within him — and there were his mathematical studies to be pursued when the allure of salons and actresses' boudoirs lost their sway. His choice was, sensibly, to retain a military link while focusing, for the moment, on his scientific studies.

Using connections in Picardy, Bougainville secured for himself the post of *aide-major*, a staff role, with the Régiment de Picardie in 1753. This left him time to work on his second volume of his treatise on integral calculus and plunge back into the heady Parisian social whirl. The Hérault de Séchelles family's influence on Bougainville's behalf did not cease, however, and either at his request or due to the family's perception that this bright light should not be hidden under a bushel, Moreau de Séchelles secured for Bougainville and Jean-Baptiste appointments in 1754 as *enseignes en pied* in the service of General François de Chevert, who commanded a military encampment at Sarrelouis, north of Nancy. Service under de Chevert was a plum posting for ambitious young officers, as he was one of the few officers of the time who viewed the study of tactics as a science. The experience was a kind of awakening for Bougainville: the delight he took in the precision and logic of mathematics now was equalled by delight in the professionalism of de Chevert's instruction in the intricacies of military manoeuvre, and it injected into Bougainville a similar professionalism of approach to the military career that replaced the light-hearted expediency of his *mousquetaires noirs* enlistment. It was a seriousness he never lost thereafter, in an age when a diffident amateurishness was a fashionable military attitude for all officers save those of the engineers and artillery.

Bougainville did not remain long at Sarrelouis, however. Catherine Hérault de Séchelles, determined to see better things for her charming and gifted proxy son, used her influence, with the support of Bougainville's uncle, Jean Potentin d'Arboulin — *La Pompadour's* "Bou-bou" — to have Bougainville appointed to an important diplomatic mission. He was made third secretary in the retinue of the Marquis de Lévis-Mirepoix, who was sent in 1754 to the Court of Saint James in London to attempt a resolution of colonial boundary issues in North America, where flintlocks were already banging away in the forest gloom over claims of territoriality. It was the first opening of Bougainville's eyes, however imperfectly, to the realities of geopolitical struggle in the wider world — and to the culture and language of the English. As a recent biographer, Mary Kimbrough, expresses it:

> Although many of the geographical problems Bougainville studied in France pertained to the sea, the ones he was to be exposed to in London dealt mainly with land areas in North America. The continent was still imperfectly mapped, and the joint British-French commission had to determine the frontiers between Acadia and Nova Scotia, and the limits between New France and the British colonies, more particularly the Ohio River basin. This was Bougainville's first introduction to the New World, but it was purely intellectual. In spite of calculating latitudes and longitudes, he never seemed to grasp the veritable immensity of the continent. It was

during his rather short stay in the British capital that Bougainville learned English, and evidently learned it well. There would be numerous occasions later on in his life when he would be sent to treat with the British foe or American friend because of his command of English.[4]

If Bougainville came away, as Kimbrough claims, from the three-month experience in London with an imperfect idea of the size of North America, he had managed an astonishing fluency in English while introducing himself to the membership of the Royal Society, who were impressed with his studies of integral calculus. He had also realized that knowledge of geographical issues and cartography, another abiding interest, had to be gained "in the field," as it were — had Freret not gone to Lapland? — and not from poring over incorrect charts on desktops. By the time the diplomatic mission ended in early 1755, with indifferent results, Bougainville had returned to France having made some key decisions for his future.

To Madame Hérault de Séchelles he confided that it was evident that France would be formally at war with England within months, and that the struggle would be worldwide in nature. The practice of law, to which he was entitled, held no attraction for him. Perhaps not surprisingly, devotion to the study of mathematics and a purely intellectual life would also not satisfy him, however good he was at that sort of thing. He had determined, as his English alter ego James Cook was doing at about the same time on the other side of the Channel, that his fortune lay in the active life of the king's service. It would be, he told *chère maman*, a soldier's life. The military authorities were only too happy to agree, and Bougainville found himself promoted to lieutenant, attached to a dragoon regiment — a sort of mounted heavy infantry — and sent off to rejoin the staff of François de Chevert at Richemont, where de Chevert maintained a second military training camp. There, Bougainville threw himself into the pursuit of mastery of the military arts with such zeal that by early 1756 he was promoted to *capitaine*. His scientific pursuits, now an avocation more than a profession, were not wholly abandoned; it was while he was at Richemont that his treatise on calculus appeared in print in France, to be published in London by his admiring colleagues at the Royal Society soon after he had received his captaincy. On January 8, 1756, he had been honoured by that same Royal Society with election to its membership.[5]

The key event in his life, which would set him on a road that was to lead to the moccasin trails of North America's forests and on to the coral reefs of the South Pacific, now took place. Catherine Hérault de Séchelles, intent that Bougainville should have an appointment that might match both his talents and his prospects, secured for him the position of aide-de-camp to Louis-Joseph de Montcalm-Gozon, Marquis de Saint-Véran. Montcalm had been selected by the minister of war, the Comte d'Argenson, to replace Baron Dieskau as French military commander in North America and would soon sail to take up his post. With him, Bougainville would voyage to Canada and the beginnings of a career he could scarcely have imagined.[6]

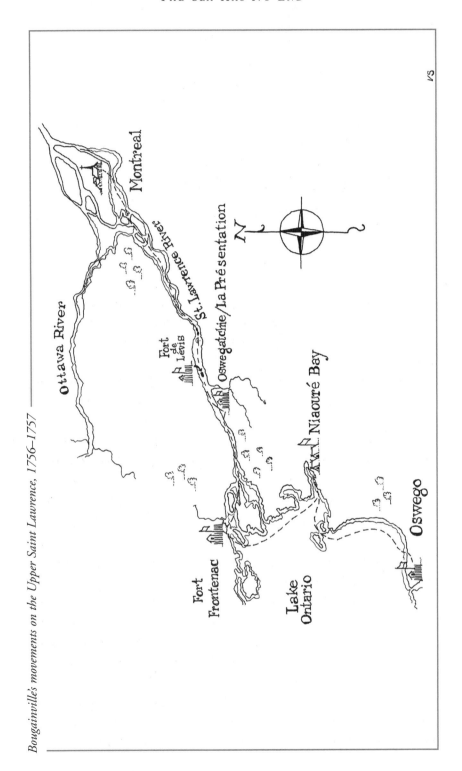

Bougainville's movements on the Upper Saint Lawrence, 1756–1757

Montreal

Ottawa River

St. Lawrence River

Fort
de
Lévis

Oswegatchie/La Présentation

Niaouré Bay

Oswego

Fort
Frontenac

Lake
Ontario

N

Chapter Two

The Seven Years' War and the Appointment to Canada

When Louis-Antoine de Bougainville sailed from Brest with Montcalm aboard the French frigate *La Licorne* on April 3, 1756, he was about to enter a North American struggle between France and Britain that was taking place at the same time that most of the significant powers within Europe were engaging in what came to be known as the Seven Years' War. These conflagrations were to become the most significant in a long period of ill will between the French and British that had begun in earnest in the 1690s and would not end until the crushing of Napoleon in 1815. The North American phase of this double war, known to the American colonists as the French and Indian War, lasted in practical terms from 1754 to 1763.

At its start, the war was a competition between France and Britain for dominance in North America and India. Gradually, more European states became involved, and the general chaos did not end until 1763. The results were a weakening of France and ascendancy for Prussia as the most influential land power in Europe. When the worldwide conflict was over, Britain was astonished to find it had won virtually a global empire at the expense of its French rival. In the broadest of summaries, the struggle between the French and British had begun in North America almost two years before *La Licorne* sailed. The British colonies along the eastern seaboard were increasingly in conflict with the crescent of French control or claims over lands that swept from Louisbourg, on remote, fog-shrouded Cape Breton Island, down the St. Lawrence, Ohio and Mississippi valleys, to the steaming lowlands of New Orleans. At stake was the simple question of which nation, and which vision of European civilization, would rule the heartland of North America.

The Ohio Valley had become the more immediate theatre of conflict, as the inhabitants of Virginia and Pennsylvania were determined that the valley was theirs for settlement or trade, while the French considered it part of New France. The British had been first to lay claim to North American soil, dating back to the voyages of John Cabot in 1497, but had in fact only put themselves ashore along the eastern seaboard and in isolated Hudson's Bay Company posts. The French, meanwhile, after Jacques Cartier's 1534 landing, had finally established themselves at Quebec in 1608, and had been far ahead of the British in exploring inland. The Sieur de la Salle's explorations of the 1680s, which encompassed the great arc between Quebec and the mouth of the Mississippi, resulted in his claiming for France the valley of the Mississippi and all the lands drained by it and its tributaries — in a nutshell, virtually everything west of the Appalachian Mountains, including the lush Ohio Valley.

The argument over which flag had the right to fly over this territory remained unresolved for more than half a century while New France and the British colonies established themselves and began to grow. In firm control of what would later be called Canada, the French began in the 1700s to expand their fur trade into the Great Lakes and down the Ohio and Mississippi rivers. The Vérendrye brothers travelled as far as the Rocky Mountains, and small but permanent settlements were established in the interior, at Detroit (in 1701); at the juncture of the Ohio and the Mississippi, where Cairo, Illinois, now exists; along the Mississippi to its mouth; and even along the coast of the Gulf of Mexico. By the 1750s, the French had also established trade and formed alliances with northern Indians, who welcomed them for their apparent lack of interest in Indian lands and their very real interest in trading. Although claimed by France, the Ohio Valley was not visited by French traders to any extent, but the French were increasingly aware of those from the British colonies across the Appalachians who were trading in the area, and who had very real designs on settlement.

The British, meanwhile, had established themselves in fourteen coastal colonies stretching from Nova Scotia to Georgia, and were already far more numerous than the small population of New France. As the eighteenth century progressed, the line of settlement of the British colonies pushed westward from the coastal lands to the mountain barrier. By 1750, in the two largest colonies, Virginia and Pennsylvania, which were the bases for influential families with a direct financial interest in claiming and exploiting the riches of the Ohio Valley, groups of settlers were beginning to appear in the various gaps in the mountains that led inland to the Ohio. And in the Indian villages of that area, scores of British traders had appeared, particularly along the upper Ohio River. To the French at Quebec, the ramifications of these inroads were all too obvious. It would be necessary to stake, and, if it came to it, defend, France's claim to the lands west of the Appalachians.

The first attempt to seal off the British behind their mountains came almost immediately after the close of the War of 1739–1748 had given France better terms than it might have expected, including the return of the fortress of Louisbourg, taken four years earlier by an enthusiastic amateur army of New Englanders. Céloron de Bienville led a party of Canadian troops and Indian allies into the Ohio Valley, where he confronted Pennsylvanian traders he found in the Ohio Indian villages and demanded that they pull down the British flags fluttering over their lean-tos and pull back across the Appalachians. The traders agreed, but once the French had vanished along the forest trails, they largely ignored the order. Three years later, another French party entered the area, but this time took forceful action, destroying the British trading centre at Pickawillany, on the Miami River, a western tributary of the Ohio, and hunting down every British trader who could be found along the banks of the Ohio. The effect of this blow upon Pennsylvania and Virginia was immediate.

The government of Virginia had long held that the Royal Charter of 1609 clearly spelled out Virginia's claim to western lands, one that the French, with some justification, disputed. By the 1750s, Virginia had handed out some one and a half million acres in the Ohio Valley to wealthy and important families — including that of George Washington. When the colony learned that the French had driven traders out of the Ohio Valley and were building posts such as Fort Presqu'Île on Lake Erie and Fort Le Boeuf on French Creek on the upper reaches of the Ohio River, it determined that the French had to be informed of the legal basis, as far as the British Crown was concerned, of the Virginia settlers' claims, and that the construction of French forts on Virginian land was illegitimate. Robert Dinwiddie, the lieutenant-governor of Virginia, therefore decided to establish a comparable British presence in the Ohio Valley. The Ohio Company was created and granted a large parcel of upper Ohio Valley land, where it was urged to build a fortified post that the colony promised to garrison. The location was to be at the junction of the Allegheny and Monongahela rivers, where Pittsburgh now stands. It was near here that the first serious fighting in what came to be known in North America as the French and Indian War would take place.

In 1754, the Ohio Company duly sent off a party of workmen to the Pittsburgh site, intent on building what they would call Fort Prince George. Alerted to these intentions, the French had dispatched a powerful little force of colonial troops, the *Compagnies franches de la Marine,* and allied warriors. The Ohio Company's men were barely into their work, and not yet under the protection of colony troops — a column of these Virginians, under Colonel Joshua Fry and his second, George Washington, was marching toward the site — when the French emerged from the forest gloom. The English workmen sensibly agreed to retire from the unfinished fortification, selling their tools to the French, who used them to complete the work. They named it Fort Duquesne after Ange Duquesne de Menneville, the governor general of Canada.

The French then sent off a small party under a young colony officer, Joseph Coulon de Villiers de Jumonville, to inform the advancing Virginians that they were intruding into lands France intended to retain, and should peaceably retire. The leadership of the Virginian column had changed, however: Fry had died unexpectedly, leaving George Washington in command. Washington's scouts reported the location of Jumonville's party, and, without waiting to determine their intent, Washington attacked the French in their camp, killing Jumonville and inflicting other casualties. That France and Britain were officially at peace was not lost on Contrecoeur, the new commandant at Fort Duquesne. Incensed at Washington's action, Contrecoeur sent off a party of five hundred French and accompanying warriors to confront Washington. The Virginians were cornered in a rudimentary little palisade named Fort Necessity, and Washington was forced to surrender after a rain-soaked and hopeless resistance.

The echoes of those sputtering and soggy musket volleys over a boggy Ohio forest meadow announced that Washington had precipitated the beginning of formal war in North America between France and Britain, spreading from Ohio to everywhere in the world that French and British interests clashed. Mirepoix's three-month diplomatic efforts in London may have provided Bougainville with the opportunity to master English and gain an entry into the Royal Society, but it failed to stop the bloody and ferocious war that was about to ensue, and Bougainville was to become caught up in it as a principal player.

The British government was initially reluctant to act upon appeals from the smarting Virginians for the dispatch of regular soldiery with which to confront the French. But with the collapse of the Mirepoix negotiations, and the reality that the colonial militias felt incapable of dealing with the less numerous, but formidable, French — who were composed mainly of Canadian colony troops and their allies from the Five Nations of the Canadian Iroquois and other tribes — the Crown agreed to send a force of British regular infantry to drive the French from the forks of the Ohio, the site of the newly completed Fort Duquesne. The British force's command was given to Major General Edward Braddock. At the same time, a strong naval force under Admiral Boscawen was sent to the approaches of the St. Lawrence to prevent any French attempts to send troops to Canada. With this commitment of permanent military and naval forces to North America, France and Britain were soon locked in what was nearly a global war, as was soon made evident when France, allying itself with Austria, attacked Hanover, which was George II's "electorate" in Europe. This was not to be a mere flintlock skirmish in the distant gloom of New World forests.

As France deployed its smaller resources with intelligence and initiative, Britain found itself needing to establish a military and naval presence in India, along the African coast, and in the West Indies and North America, while protecting Hanover in the hopes that it would not be swallowed up in the dramatic German struggle on the continent. For the first while, however, Britain and its colonies were put very much on the losing end of things. From 1754 until 1758, the French found that, with few exceptions, they could do no wrong in the far-flung frontier war in North America. Against the British colonial militias and the regulars sent to help them, the small garrison of Canada and its warrior allies enjoyed dramatic success, and not only did the British claim to the Ohio seem a forlorn hope, but France hoped it might successfully prevent any expansion of the British settlements from their narrow coastal strip along the Atlantic coast.

The string of initial successes for the French — in actual terms a triumvirate of European French regular troops, Canadian colonial troops and Indian allies — began in 1755 with the defeat of General Braddock's force of regular and colonial infantry, which was ambushed as it approached Fort Duquesne. Nearing the forks of the Ohio in a ponderous, regulated column that literally hacked its own road out of the forest as it approached, Braddock's force was surrounded and cut to pieces on July 9, 1755, by a forest-savvy French force that fought, warrior-style, from the shelter of the trees, shooting down the massed ranks of redcoats where they stood. In the next year, a small post established by the English on Lake Ontario's south shore, at Oswego, was taken by the newly arrived Montcalm, with Bougainville present. This was followed in

1757 by Montcalm's capture of Fort William Henry, at the lower end of Lake George in what is now New York state. Present at this event as well, Bougainville was sent away with dispatches before the surrendering British garrison marched out of the surrounded fort on its way south, only to be attacked and mauled by the Indian warriors accompanying the French troops. The warriors had their own wartime agenda, and were intent on securing prisoners for sale or adoption. The cruelty that accompanied this act — sick or wounded prisoners were simply slain — was repeated in thousands of isolated cases where lone cabins or villages, both white and Indian, were set upon by brutal men of both origins who spared no one who could not survive the march back to captivity. The ruthlessness of the war, as fought by the warrior allies of the French, exposed the impressionable Bougainville to horrors ranging from torture to ritual cannibalism.

Also in 1757, a British attempt to mount a seaborne assault on the fortress of Louisbourg on Cape Breton Island failed to materialize. In the year that followed, France appeared to have the upper hand: the exposed British posts on the edge of French territory had been taken and destroyed, and the core of New France was secure. British traders and settlers west of the Alleghenies continued to be driven off the disputed lands or killed in 1758, and in the most significant success of the year, at which Bougainville was present, the army of General James Abercromby, attacking the key French fort at Carillon, or Ticonderoga, at the southern end of Lake Champlain, was shattered on July 8 by the defending garrison under Montcalm and forced to flee south in a humiliating rout.

In these years, the British had scored some victories. In the Champlain Valley, a French regular and militia force under Montcalm's predecessor as New France's military commander, the Saxon officer Jean-Armand, Baron Dieskau, had marched south in September 1755 after it was learned that the English were planning to attack the French post at Fort Saint-Frédéric, or Crown Point, just to the north of Carillon on Lake Champlain. The British force was in fact composed of colonial militia under the command of a skilled Mohawk Valley landowner named William Johnson. On their way north, the British halted to set up camp and were attacked by Dieskau's force. Their resistance and counterattack was so effective, however, that the French sustained heavy losses and Dieskau was wounded and taken prisoner, a loss that led to Montcalm's appointment.

Again in 1755, the French were forced to give up Fort Beauséjour, which they had built on the Isthmus of Chignecto, the narrow neck of land that anchors Nova Scotia to the mainland, or what would become New Brunswick. France had rejected British claims to the area after 1713, citing one of its own dating back to the 1600s, and the area had been settled by Acadian French farmers who tried to maintain a naïve neutrality in the midst of the great struggle. Fort Beauséjour had served as a symbol to the Acadians, and the British not only took it, but also forced the evacuation of the Acadians by sea, dispersing them to the British colonies to the south. Unwelcome there, many found themselves in Louisiana, where their "Cajun" descendants remain to this day. Nova Scotia passed in fact as well as legality into British hands.

By 1758, while the French were more than holding their own, the British government was coming to an understanding that the court of Louis XV and his administration in New France appreciated less fully: that the most important fight was not the land war in Europe, in all its Byzantine complexity, nor even the struggle for supremacy in India; it was the struggle for the destiny of North America. This realization came to be reflected concretely in the policies of Prime Minister William Pitt, and the French would watch with concern his efforts to take personal control of virtually every aspect of the war, reorganizing and revitalizing his nation's strategy in a way that would lead ultimately to British victory in North America.

The first ominous signs of reversal began to appear at sea, as the Royal Navy gradually gained dominance over *la marine royale* of Louis XV. By 1759, French merchant shipping had been disastrously curtailed. Then, two major defeats at the hands of the Royal Navy virtually destroyed France's naval power, which would leave the Canadian colonies cut off from supplies and fresh troops; these were the defeat of the French Mediterranean Fleet off Lagos, Portugal, by Admiral Boscawen, and the near destruction of France's Atlantic forces in Quiberon Bay by Admiral Edward Hawke. The North American land war had been going well for France to this point, but these naval defeats announced that the French forces in Canada would be without food — the colony could not feed everyone — reinforcements or munitions, while the British regular regiments and colonial militias could be supplied by the healthy and self-sufficient American colonies, which were already enjoying a standard of living far above that of Europe.

As the situation began to turn in Britain's favour, France was unable to make any major new commitment to the North American War. The British Parliament, on the other hand, voted huge sums to support Pitt's strategy and offered the American colonies financial incentives should they defeat the French. The introduction of prudent Dutch financial methods into the governmental process by William of Orange at the end of the seventeenth century had prepared Britain to fund and manage such expenditures; the task was, meanwhile, beyond the capacity of France's feudal economy. Armed with financial might, Pitt now rebuilt and strengthened the army, ensuring that new and competent commanders replaced such lesser lights as Abercromby. The British regiments in North America, and the colonial militias supporting them, still sought a military resolution by means of traditional, European-style confrontation in the field. But the French had been finding that the British were becoming disturbingly adept at the skulking, irregular forest warfare that Bougainville came to know as *la petite guerre* — "the little war." Backed by the Royal Navy's success at sea, supported by the food and supplies of the colonies, and led by competent men handpicked and carefully overseen by Prime Minister Pitt, the British were ready to bring to an end their long string of losses in North America.

The French were soon made aware that Pitt had devised a strategy that called for a simultaneous assault on four fronts: against Louisbourg in the east, and into the mouth of the St. Lawrence toward Quebec; up the Champlain Valley, against Carillon and Fort Saint-Frédéric, and up the Richelieu River — the "dagger aimed at the heart of Canada"; against the Ohio forts, then to Oswego and down the St. Lawrence to Montreal; and against Fort Niagara, which controlled the mouth of the Niagara River and the great hinterland to the south and west. To the growing dismay of the French and the almost equal astonishment of the British, Pitt's grand strategy worked flawlessly, with only seasonal delays.

Commencing with the capture of Louisbourg in 1758, the key posts on all fronts were taken one by one until, in September 1759, the ten minutes of devastating volleys of Wolfe's army led to the fall of Quebec at the Battle of the Plains of Abraham, where Bougainville, caught unawares upriver by the British assault, lost his mentor, friend and commander, Montcalm. The British held on to Quebec over the winter of 1759–60, and in 1760 the French retreated under pressure from east and west to their last stronghold, Montreal, Bougainville briefly commanding the garrison at Île-aux-Noix on the Richelieu. It was in Montreal, on September 8, 1760, that the Marquis de Vaudreuil, governor of New France, surrendered his colony — and France's aspirations in North America — to the British army waiting outside the city gates. It fell to Bougainville, with his fluency in English, to negotiate the terms of the surrender. The last significant events of the war in the Western Hemisphere occurred with the 1762 defeat of a small French force put ashore in Newfoundland and the capture of Havana, a prize that would later be exchanged for Florida, that same year by a British assault force. The peace treaty followed a year later, signed in Paris on February 10, 1763.[1]

Only a few swatches of colour had yet been applied to this broad canvas of conflict when Bougainville came to North America. On January 25, 1756, Montcalm had received a letter from the war minister, d'Argenson, informing him that Louis XV "has chosen you to command his troops in North America, and will honour you on your departure with the rank of major general."[2]

The departure process was a tedious one, and it was not until the end of March that the voyage could begin. Montcalm had met Bougainville, one of his three aides-de-camp, and had been pleased with what he saw ("a man of parts, and pleasant company"). The force that was to travel with Montcalm assembled at Brest, along with his second and third in command, Lévis and Bourlamaque, and went aboard a six-ship squadron in which Bougainville was to receive his first taste of the sea. It consisted of three frigates, *La Licorne*, *Le Sauvage* and *La Sirène*, and three larger warships rendered into transports (*en flûte*) to carry the soldiery: *L'Héros*, *L'Illustre* and *Le Léopard*. Francis Parkman records the scene and Bougainville's reaction:

> The troops destined for Canada were only two battalions, one belonging to the Regiment of La Sarre, and the other to that of Royal Roussillon. Louis XV and Pompadour sent a hundred thousand men to fight the battles of Austria, and could spare but twelve hundred to reinforce New France. These troops marched into Brest at early morning, breakfasted in the town, and went at once aboard the transports, "with an incredible gaiety," says Bougainville. "What a nation is ours! Happy he who commands it, and commands it worthily!" Montcalm and Bougainville embarked in the "Licorne," and sailed on the third of April, leaving Lévis and Bourlamaque to follow a few days later.[3]

With such enthusiasm buoying him, Louis-Antoine de Bougainville had embarked on the chapter of his life that would be at once the most dangerous and the most formative. And it would take place in the gloom of the primeval forests, or on the silvered lakes and rivers, of a continent that was as yet a mystery to him. As he sailed, Bougainville revealed both a charm and an optimism that would remain a distinctive quality of his character to the end of his astonishing life. It is difficult not to like him.

I am delighted with my general [Montcalm]. He is friendly, witty, frank and open-minded. I have every reason to believe that he likes me. He hides nothing from me and pays me the honour of consulting me, an honour I repay by not advising him! He is very keen to put my humble services to use and I am happy to oblige. What more can I want? We are at the moment hove-to awaiting a favourable wind. The captain of *La Licorne*, M. le Chevalier de Rigaudière, is very friendly and a most distinguished officer.... He has promised to teach me as much as possible about seamanship and navigation during our crossing ...[4]

The dream of seeing what lay beyond the horizon, learned at the elbow of his brother and poring over maps and charts of an exotic and distant world, was becoming a reality.

Chapter Three

Forest Warfare and the Canadian Journals, 1756–1758

When Bougainville arrived in Canada on May 12, 1756, he had had the experience of marvelling at the thousand-mile passage inland to Quebec as east winds pushed the frigate past the sweeping, forested, mountainous north shore and rolling south shore until it anchored below the great rock of Quebec. But he was afforded little time to develop an appreciation for the beauty and social life of the little garrison capital: within two weeks he was embarked in one of "the King's canoes" for Montreal, where he was immersed in staff work in the little walled town while Montcalm went on to inspect the fortifications at Carillon (Ticonderoga) at the southern end of Lake Champlain. His unusual and growing interest in naval affairs was stirred by a report from Lake Ontario, and his formal journal entry reveals a small disdainfulness for English valour afloat:

> Received news of the taking of an English shallop, armed with nine swivels, on Lake Ontario, our armed craft met those of the English on their first reconnaissance. The English manoeuvred to give chase, but, seeing us advance instead of turning tail, they fled. Maxim of the English at sea: avoid combat when only on equal or slightly superior terms on the same principle that one gives one's purse to any thief that demands it, even in a public place and within reach of

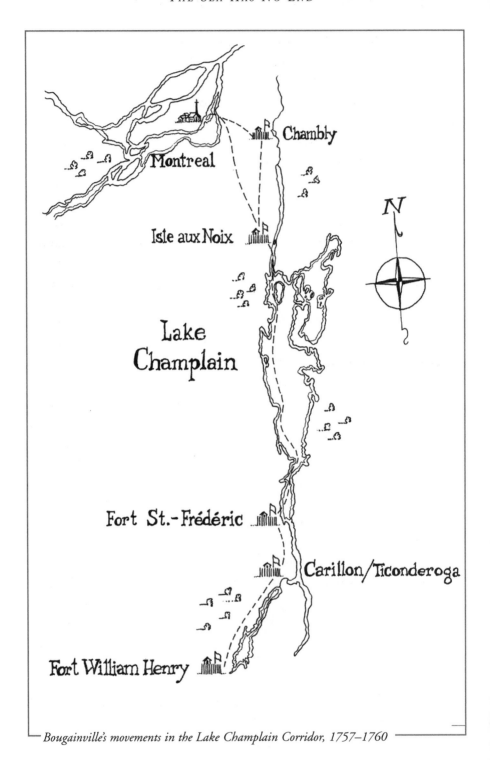

Bougainville's movements in the Lake Champlain Corridor, 1757–1760

help. The crew, to a number of sixteen men, has been sent to Quebec. A petty victory like all achieved in this country, but interesting because of the impression of superiority that it gives our Indians.[1]

By mid July it was evident that the governor of Canada, the Marquis de Vaudreuil, had determined to make an attack on the English outpost of Oswego, on the south shore of Lake Ontario, by which the English were gaining access to the lake from the Mohawk Valley and Oneida Lake. Montcalm, a military commander required to defer to the governor's overall leadership, agreed with some reluctance to Vaudreuil's insistence that this be his first mission. Montcalm would have preferred to approach the task in terms of a traditional European siege employing regular metropolitan (European) troops. But he soon found that the governor, Canadian-born and mindful of the value of Indian-style warfare, wished him to make far greater use of warrior allies and Canadian troops than his regular regiments.

For Vaudreuil, the guerrilla-style forest warfare practised by the warrior allies — and which the Canadians referred to as *la petite guerre* — had been the guarantor of New France's survival in the unending conflict with the more numerous English colonists to the south. Vaudreuil had observed that "nothing is more calculated to disgust the people of those [British] colonies and to make them desire the return of peace" than the hidden war of ambush and sudden strike against frontier settlements, a brand of war most suited to the warriors' capabilities.[2]

Montcalm's disagreement with Vaudreuil went deeper, with aspects of civil-military rivalry and tension between the Old World and the New. It would form the basis of a lasting enmity between the two men that would only end with Montcalm's death and the loss of Canada. It was a conflict that placed Bougainville squarely in the middle of a tactical and strategic disagreement of major proportions.

As almost any conventional minded European regular officer would have, Montcalm disliked departures from what he understood to be civilized standards of

military conduct. He distrusted Indians, who oper-
ated according to their own understandings of warfare
and could not be subjected to military discipline.
Because Indians sought to gain prisoners, trophies and
booty, they could be ungovernable in the aftermath of
a battle and were particularly prone to what Montcalm
could only understand as acts of savagery — scalping,
torture, even cannibalism. But most important, to use
Indians seemed futile to Montcalm because no matter
how many small victories they might win, they could
inflict no lasting defeat on the British; once a battle
had been won, they would simply take their captives
and loot and return home. So far as Montcalm could
see, the Canadian militia and even the [regular colony
troops] were only marginally preferable to the Indians,
since whatever their skills in woodcraft, neither could
compare with properly disciplined European troops in
reliability under fire or staying power.[3]

Bougainville's intelligence and common sense would lead him to
a growing appreciation of North American methods of fighting, as he
experienced it and absorbed its lessons — this would be evident in
1759 — but he could never bring himself consciously to divorce
himself from the regular officer's principles of professionalism
expressed by Montcalm. This placed him on Montcalm's side, both
professionally and in terms of the Canadian–versus–Metropolitan
French rivalry. It was a more comforting position than the matter-of-
fact acceptance of frontier savagery which seemed to be the Canadian
view. And for Bougainville, even as he came to establish a remarkable
intimacy with, and knowledge of, Indian society, he could never
overcome his unease at the nature of the "little war" of the warrior
and the Canadian who fought the same way.

But this grim awareness lay yet in the future. For the moment,
Bougainville was immersed in staff work at Montreal for the pending
effort against Oswego, and on July 11 he had his first close observation
of warriors, watching a band of Menominee who had arrived from

distant Lake Michigan with several English prisoners, around whom they proceeded to dance before the governor, Vaudreuil.

> Extraordinary spectacle, more suited to terrify than to please; curious, however, to the eye of a philosopher who seeks to study Man in conditions nearest to nature. These men were naked save for a piece of cloth in front and behind, the face and body painted, feathers on their heads, symbol and signal for war, tomahawk and spear in their hand. In general these are all brawny men, large and of good appearance; almost all are very greasy...[4]

On July 21, 1756, Bougainville left Montreal with Montcalm to travel upriver toward Fort Frontenac — the site of modern-day Kingston, Ontario — and join with the force that would attack Oswego, or Chouaguen, as it was known to the Indians. The passage, by way of the thriving French outpost and Christian Iroquois settlement of Fort La Présentation or Oswegatchie — now Ogdensburg, New York — took eight days, with Bougainville's canoe arriving at Fort Frontenac at ten o'clock on the morning of July 29.[5]

From Frontenac, Montcalm moved his large force to Niaoure Bay, to the south of the opening down the St. Lawrence River from Lake Ontario. Niaoure Bay was a small French stockaded post which in another half-century would be known as Sackets Harbor, the Lake Ontario base of the United States Navy during the War of 1812. In 1756, however, it held on its shores the hundreds of *bateaux* and canoes of Montcalm's force, consisting of just under three thousand French regular infantry, artillerymen and militia, and some 250 warriors of tribes allied to France, in addition to engineers, tradesmen of all kinds and militia labourers to help with the work of a formal siege.[6]

It was here that Bougainville witnessed the first great "council," the formal, circular formation in which warrior chiefs or their selected orators rose in turn to debate before Montcalm the issues concerning the coming fight. For Montcalm and Bougainville, the explanation by a Nipissing chief of the warriors' attitude toward European war against forts was unequivocal.

> [We ask you] never to expose the Natives to the fire of artillery and musketry from the forts, since their custom was never to fight against entrenchments or stockades, but in the forest where they understood war, and where they could find trees for cover.[7]

Montcalm agreed to respect the warriors' views, and indicated that the main assault against Oswego's fortifications would be made by the French troops, with the warriors to be used for scouting and other peripheral duties. Back in Quebec, Vaudreuil would have wished the preponderance of the assault force to have been warriors, and had sent invitations to hundreds of villages of Great Lakes nations to take part. Only the threat of smallpox, reported at Niagara, had prevented the warriors from coming east to present Montcalm with a largely Indian force to lead against a fort they would not have agreed to attack.[8]

Oswego was a small, stockaded post built on the left, or western side of the mouth of the Oswego River where it emptied northward into the bleak chill of Lake Ontario. It was an inadequate and crumbling structure dominated by high land to either side of the river mouth. To rectify this situation, the English had built a small fort slightly farther west, on higher land, which they called Fort George, or "new Fort Oswego," and a sizable fortification on a commanding height on the east side of the river mouth, which was named Fort Ontario. The original small post on low land at the river's edge had been improved with low, fortified walls to make a sort of enclosed, defensible camp. It was against this position that Montcalm sent off his force in two divisions, in a great flotilla of *bateaux* and canoes that coasted westward from Naioure Bay in early August. By August 10, an advance party of Canadian colonial troops, militia and warriors arrived just east of Oswego and set up a defensive screen behind which the first half of Montcalm's force, the infantry, got ashore. The second half, the larger boats and vessels carrying the artillery, heavy equipment and Montcalm himself, arrived on August 12. With warriors showing the way, the French moved to besiege their first objective, Fort Ontario.[9]

For Bougainville, there was a sudden immersion into the fighting arts of the warriors, as Montcalm released him to fall in with the advance guard, which had been led by the charismatic Nipissing chief Kisensik.[10] This meant laying aside the lace and small sword of the staff officer and dressing in the manner of the Canadians who fought with the warriors: a sleeved waistcoat or uniform coat with docked skirts; buckskin leggings or infantry gaiters to above the knee; a knapsack and water gourd slung over one shoulder and a cartridge box and priming horn over the other; a waistbelt to hold a knife or tomahawk thrust in at the small of the back; a light officer's flintlock musket cradled in his arm; and a plain cocked hat worn over his own unpowdered hair, simply tied. It was a far cry from the elegant dress of a Parisian salon, and in it Bougainville was abruptly introduced to the exhausting, woods-ranging warrior way of fighting as few French metropolitan officers would be, plunging into the woods surrounding Oswego alongside Nipissing, Abenaki, Algonquin and Christian Iroquois warriors. The stocky athleticism of his youthful days with Jean-Baptiste Hérault de Séchelles would now be tested in depth.

The advance party soon found its way to a small bay named *La Petite Anse*, now Baldwin's Bay, about a mile and a half to the east of Oswego, that was deemed suitable for landing the main body of Montcalm's force and the artillery. Bougainville relates the beginning of the action in the third person:

> The advance guard ... left at ten on foot to go through the woods without being seen to take a position at La Petite Anse to cover the landing of the first division, which should start moving at seven this evening in order to arrive during the night.[11]

The next morning, August 11, after lying on their arms in the forest overnight, Bougainville's warriors and Canadians were led by Kisensik to within musket shot of Fort Ontario, a¹ ¹ began sniping from the shelter of the forest at the English garrison within. The

English replied, blazing away spiritedly with eight guns and a small mortar, providing Bougainville with his first taste of actual fire. He proved equal to the test, leading Montcalm to comment afterward:

> You would not believe the resources I find in [Bougainville].... [H]e exposes himself readily to gunfire, a matter on which he needs to be restrained rather than encouraged. I shall be much mistaken if he does not have a good head for soldiering.[12]

With more French infantry ashore, the advance party now came under the command of François-Pierre de Rigaud de Vaudreuil, a tough colonial officer as steely and direct as his brother the governor was not. From August 11 until the morning of August 13, Rigaud kept the little advance force hovering about Fort Ontario to screen the activity behind them, dodging round shot as it came bowling round them through the trees, and replying with whoops and a hail of musketry which, "although [it] did not kill a soul, it tied down the enemy, fearful for their scalps, and gave great confidence to our soldiers."[13]

The regular French troops and their militia labourers, meanwhile, had been busily digging away at the gun positions and entrenchments behind Bougainville's party, on the long slope to the east of Fort Ontario. The planned bombardment proved unnecessary, however; late in the afternoon of August 13 the fort's guns fell suddenly silent. A small party sent forward by Rigaud to peer over the walls came lathering back to report the garrison had evacuated the fort. Montcalm's regulars immediately dragged the guns forward to employ the heights of Fort Ontario to bombard Fort George and the palisaded camp on the opposite side of the river, to which the Fort Ontario garrison had fled. They hoped to be ready to open fire by dawn of August.[14]

The English commandant, Mercer, was not about to surrender without a fight; the guns he had in the fortified camp surrounding the original post of Oswego were swung round from their westward-facing position and began blasting away at the French on the Fort Ontario heights. Night fell, and Montcalm's gunners and labourers toiled away by torch and lantern light in the summer heat as round shot hurtled in amongst them out of the darkness. Bougainville relates both that fire's effect and what transpired next:

> The enemy fired briskly during the entire night, and especially toward morning. Our battery was very late in firing, and then only with a few pieces. M. de Rigaud [was] ordered to go with the Canadians and Indians and cross the river three-quarters of a league upstream and to harass the enemy. I have been detached to cross the river with him and at noon to summon the enemy to surrender.[14]

This crossing westward over the Oswego River was not an easy manoeuvre; there were several English vessels anchored in the river near its mouth that were able to turn their guns on Bougainville's party and whose shot hummed past overhead or threw up towering, drenching geysers as the French entered the river. The current was fast, and Rigaud led them resolutely across under this bombardment — with some swimming, others (including Bougainville) wading in water up to their necks in places, holding muskets, powder horns and cartridge boxes over their heads. Once ashore, the fearsome little force squelched northward again toward the fortified camp, then swung west to approach the "new" fort, which was so badly built and indefensible that the garrison called it "Fort Rascal."

Fort Rascal it may have been, but it was where Mercer had intended to withdraw from the old post for a last stand. As the cannonading went on, and Rigaud's move was seen, the contest ceased abruptly to be in doubt.

> According to Stephen Cross, a civilian carpenter who had come to Oswego to build ships, what followed was "as Severe a Cannonade on Both Sides, as Perhaps Ever was, until about 10 o'clock." Then, Cross continued, "about this time we Discovered the Enemy, in Great Numbers, Crossing the River [upstream] and we

not in force Sufficient to go up and Oppose them, and being Judged not safe, any longer, to Keep the Men in Fort Raskel, that was Evacuated; and [while] we all were huddled together In and about the Main Fort, the Commandant... was killed by a Cannon Ball."[15]

The garrison and its second in command, Colonel John Littlehales, were disheartened by the death of Mercer and the crossing of Rigaud's men, and "now despair seized them, increased by the screams and entreaties of the women, of whom there were more than a hundred in the place." Within an hour of Mercer's death, Littlehales sent out two officers under a flag of truce to seek terms of surrender.[16]

Bougainville, with his command of English, was sent forward to discuss the terms. He reports it laconically:

> At nine, Colonel Mercer who commanded at Oswego was killed. An hour later the enemy hoisted a white flag, and two officers came to make proposals for surrender. I have been sent to propose the articles and to remain as a hostage. The articles are that the garrison will be prisoners of war, that the officers and soldiers ... will be taken to Montreal to be exchanged.[17]

It was an extraordinary success for Montcalm, and for the French. The haul of booty was impressive, as a prisoner's diary relates:

> A great quantity of stores [which] we suppose [amount to] about 9,000 barrels of provisions, a Considerable Number of Brass, and Iron Cannon, and Mortars; one Vessel just Launched, two Sloops Pierced for 10 guns each, one Schooner Pierced for 10 guns, and one Row Galley, with Swivels, and one Small vessel on the Stock about Half Built, a great Number of Whailboats, and as near as I can judge between 14 & 16 hundred Prisoners; including

Soldiers, Sailers, Carpenters, and other Artifisers, Settlers, Indians, traders, Women and Children.[18]

Until August 20, the French busied themselves in gathering up and sending away to Frontenac — and thence on to Montreal — the prisoners and captured goods, and in destroying Oswego's fortifications. Bougainville's journal has entries that show him off on naval work ("I have been sent to explore the coast the other side of the Oswego River, to sound the anchorages and bays suitable for a landing") and relating the departures of various elements of Montcalm's force. Nowhere, however, does it mention what happened to the English garrison upon surrender at the hanmds of the warriors. The survivor Stephen Cross relates it:

> The Indians had got into our fort [and] they went searching for Rum; which they found, and began to Drink, when they soon became like so many hell Hounds; and after Murdering, and Scalping all they Could find on that Side, Come over the River [to Fort Ontario, where Cross and most of the prisoners were being held] with a Design, to do the Same to all the Rest; and on their Coming Near the Fort where we was, and hearing the Confused noyes of those within [the walls, they] United their Hideous Yells and Rushed the [French] Guards Exceeding hard, to git in among us, with their Tomehawks; and it was with Great difficulty that the French could prevent them.[19]

Bougainville's immediate reaction to this assault, in which anywhere up to a hundred English soldiers, women and children were either murdered or made captive by the warriors alongside whom he had spent a week fighting and living, is unknown. Unlike Montcalm, he seems to have understood very early the value of warrior warfare methods in North American fighting. But again, the civilized *philosophe* and rational lover of the classics in him could never, his writings later revealed, overcome his horror at the other aspects of

49

Indian society at war, even coming as he did from a society which itself exhibited public cruelty toward criminals and the condemned to a ferocious degree. It rarely entered his journal, but in letters to his closest confidante, Madame Hérault, he poured out his dismay at what he was forced to witness and experience, as in this letter written before the 1757 campaign:

> Only with the greatest difficulty are we able to keep in check these savages from the furthermost backwoods; they are the most notorious cannibals among all the tribes and surely the most ferocious of all mankind. Listen to what their chiefs had to say to Monsieur de Montcalm three days ago. "It is no good counting on us, my father, to give quarter to the English. We have among us young braves who have not tasted of their broth. Fresh meat has brought them from the ends of the world. They must learn to handle the knife and plunge it into English hearts!" So much for our comrades, *ma chère maman*. What a rabble, what a sight for sensitive souls![20]

And shortly after, in another letter to his brother, Jean-Pierre:

> We have close upon 8,000 men, among them 1,800 naked savages, some black, some red, all yelling, shrieking, dancing, chanting war songs, getting drunk and crying for "broth," that is to say, blood, who have been lured five hundred leagues by the smell of fresh meat and the opportunity of teaching their youth how to carve up a human body for the cauldron. Such are the companions who shadow our every movement night and day.[21]

If the behaviour of the warriors after the English surrender at Oswego constituted an atrocity for Bougainville and the other Europeans, it represented no such evil for the warriors themselves, and it was this ethical and behavioral dissonance that bedevilled the relationship of the French to their warrior allies, and which came to constitute the single most important theme of Bougainville's experience of North America and its peoples. Bougainville was, if not in fact a *philosophe*, one who was attuned to the ideas that found their clearest expression in the writings of Jean-Jacques Rousseau. Essentially it held that civilization and its complexities were a hindrance to human happiness, and that in a simpler society — not necessarily a more primitive one, it should be noted — man was a happier being. To this was added Bougainville's extensive knowledge of the classics, and the Arcadian concepts of a Grecian golden age. The proof of such thinking would have been in the discovery of "uncivilized" peoples whose simplicity of society engendered a nobility of spirit and "happiness" in European terms. The Iroquois, Nipissing and Abenaki warriors alongside whose muscular, naked forms Bougainville trotted in the forest gloom or stalked the English in ambush were certainly people of a simpler society in a *philosophe's* terms, and on their own terms displayed "happiness" to the equal of Europeans, perhaps even more so per capita, although such things were not a matter of quantitative study in the eighteenth century. Yet in warfare the warriors exhibited a cruelty that, if it made sense to their world, sorely shook the concept of the nobler, simpler man in Bougainville's mind and created a gloomy dilemma he was unable to reconcile throughout his Canadian career. As will be seen, he entered into Indian society to a degree few metropolitan French officers did, and came in the end to espouse much of the warriors' views and methods of war, at least in tactics. But the gap he never closed while in Canada was that between an eighteenth-century thinker's conviction about the likely nobility of simpler societies and the soldier's horror at the ruthless practice of war by members of just such a society. The resolution of that dilemma would have to wait until his later career in the South Pacific.

Gradually, the Oswego assault force returned by sections to Montreal and Quebec. For Bougainville, the autumn held a long and arduous period of patrolling and fighting, at his own request, in the Lake George–Lake Champlain corridor as a member of small war parties of Canadians and warriors harassing the English to the south. It was a very personal war, and by the time the snow flew — and Bougainville had returned to the relative comfort of his quarters at Quebec — he was exhausted.

> I am tired out with this campaign. Since my arrival in Canada I have travelled close upon 500 leagues. The continual travelling, the poor food, the frequent lack of sleep, the nights spent under the open sky in the woods, the expeditions with the Indians, have affected my chest a little. At the end of last month I even spat blood. Diet and rest will set me up and make me fit to start off again in the spring. As far as that goes, I was by no means the only one to suffer from the hardships of the campaign.... One needs an iron constitution not to feel the effects of such endurance.[22]

The victory at Oswego proved to be a flash point for the simmering rivalry between Montcalm and Vaudreuil, which caught up Bougainville. Montcalm learned that Vaudreuil had sent off a report to Versailles that stressed his own role in creating the expedition and Rigaud's hand in securing the victory, but which virtually ignored the role of Montcalm and the regular soldiery. Incensed, Montcalm "asked Bougainville to intercede with his uncle, Jean-Potentin d'Arboulin, who in his position as a high postal official had often obliged Madame de Pompadour by intercepting her enemies' mail for her. Bougainville did as [he was] asked, and the King's mistress saw to it that Montcalm's version of the encounter was printed in the *Mercure* and the *Journal de Verdun*, two influential newssheets." It was the sort of discreditable politics that Bougainville detested, throughout the war and thereafter.[23]

The winter of 1756–57 passed for Bougainville with a healing immersion into the limited but vibrant social life of Quebec, which may, as did most periods of his life, have involved visits to the boudoirs of ladies charmed by his warmth, intelligence and now-acclaimed courageous gallantry. He was weighed down, however, by the continuing struggle between Montcalm and Vaudreuil over authority and the inefficiencies of the colonial government, and by the brutal reality of his first Canadian winter.

> January 8. This morning there fell a freezing rain accompanied by an icy wind which bit deep. The roads are impassable. One could not understand how frightful this country is if he has not been here. Minus 14 degrees. Northeast wind. Great ball and faro at the Intendant's house.[24]

Spring brought warmer weather, but a gloomy assessment of the colony's chances for survival.

> May 12–15. There is great misery in Quebec. Bread is scarce and what little there is of the worst quality. The Intendant has been obliged to distribute two thousand minots of wheat to the inhabitants for seed. This quantity is far from sufficient and part of the land will remain unsowed. They will even have to bring from the depots food intended for the troops in order to feed the capital.... The lack of provisions prevents us from starting the campaign. All thought of offensive action is impossible for us.[25]

Bougainville's alternating fascination and revulsion with the warriors and their societies ("[they are] fit subjects for a painting, almost all of great height.... Their bearing is noble and proud"[26]) led him to fill his journal with musings on their nature that returned often to comparisons with the inhabitants of the ancient, classical world:

> Each band goes and dances in its turn before the house of the principal citizens of the town. In truth, their dances seem like the pyrrhic and the other war dances of the Greeks.[27]

For much of the summer of 1757, Bougainville found himself either travelling with Montcalm or, when he could, donning the leggings and haversack of *la petite guerre* and patrolling with parties of warriors in the woods of the Champlain Valley. In mid July he moved south with Montcalm's headquarters, along the lake to Carillon (Ticonderoga) to prepare for a more formal campaign against the English posts, but not before an extraordinary event took place. Bougainville had, in contrast to many of the metropolitan French officers, developed a relationship with the warriors whose privations in the forests he had shared — notwithstanding his personal horrors — and his dogged endurance of warrior fighting ways and exhausting forays into the gloom of the great white pine forests with them had earned their respect. This, as much as political motives of the band chiefs, led to his adoption into the Christian Iroquois during a visit with Montcalm to the Akwesasne Iroquois settlement on the St. Lawrence River, on July 9. He recorded the event:

> The Iroquois adopted me during this feast and gave me the name of "Garionatsigoa," which means "Great Angry Sky." Behold me, then, an Iroquois war chief! My clan is that of the Turtle, first in eloquence but second in war, that of the Bear being first. They exhibited me to all the nation, gave me the first morsel of the war feast, and I sang my war song, in part with their first war chief.[28]

It was a considerable distance from this scene to those in which Bougainville had described warriors only in terms of horror and revulsion. In addition, though his journal discreetely makes no mention of it, there is evidence through his letters that at this time Bougainville began a relationship with a striking Indian girl named Ceuta, a displaced Ohio Valley Shawnee who now lived among the Christian Iroquois, as many subject bands to the Iroquois did. From this relationship, which Bougainville ended painfully on his departure from

Canada at the insistence of his *chère maman,* there may have been at least one child and possibly others, from whom modern families in North America can trace descent.[29]

The next major military action which loomed ahead for Bougainville was Montcalm's move to undertake a siege of Fort William Henry at the southern end of Lake George, intended to forestall a feared English thrust northward. Through the latter part of July 1757, Montcalm assembled at Carillon a mixed force which would prove to be the last great assemblage of warriors in support of French military efforts in the French and Indian War.

In Quebec, Vaudreuil had learned that the new British commander in North America, Lord Loudon, was planning an attack using his best troops, including those from New York, against the Fortress of Louisbourg or, less likely, Quebec itself. As historian D. Peter MacLeod succinctly puts it:

> This intelligence led Vaudreuil to take advantage of the temporary British weakness in New York by lunging south to take Fort William Henry. A successful siege would drive the British back over the watershed that lay between Lake George and the Hudson River and clear the way for an invasion of northern New York.... For the French, the campaign had an important strategic target that would enhance the security of Canada.[30]

The concept was to be the same as that successfully applied at Oswego. The warriors and Canadians were to form the auxiliary forces, while Montcalm's regular troops and siege equipment would form the main assault body. The advance party left Carillon on July 30 and moved south over Lake George, arriving in the vicinity of Fort William Henry on August 3. At Carillon, Bougainville had remarked with astonishment on the number and variety of warriors who had arrived there to support the attack, intent on prisoners, the capture of booty, and the harvest of war-trophy scalps. He was determined to remain observant and objective.

> As I have occasion to learn something concerning their religion, their habits, and their customs, I shall not neglect an objective important in the eyes of a philosopher, and one who studies that most essential thing of all, Man.[31]

The force that Montcalm commanded had so heavy a warrior component due to Vaudreuil's effective campaigning in the higher Great Lakes — the *pays d'en haut* — for warriors to join the fray. The reports of the warriors' destruction of Braddock in 1755, and Montcalm's own victory at Oswego, combined with stories of Montcalm's willingness to pay for English prisoners on the spot to bring warriors in numbers even Vaudreuil could not have imagined. To join his more formal army of more than 6,000 French regular troops, colony troops (the *Compagnies franches de la Marine*), and Canadian militia, Montcalm also had a wildly diverse body of about 2,000 warriors, including Abenaki, Kanawake, Nipissing, Ojibwa, Odawa, Chippewa, Mississauga, Menominee, Potawatami, Winnebago, Sauk, Fox, Miami, Delaware, and even a rarely-seen party of Iowa whom no one could understand. As more arrived, this gave him no less than thirty-three separate national and linguistic groups to deal with, which he could in no way command but only hope to persuade in the great enterprise. Bougainville was astounded.[32]

The difficulties of trying to lead such a force soon became apparent.

> The advance guard left [Carillon] on schedule, but the [warriors] of this body experienced some difficulties with their French allies during the first days of the march. First, French officers attempted to deploy most of the warriors on the right flank. The [warriors] did not find this acceptable and took their accustomed place at the head of the column. Later on, during the

night, as the Odawa were engaged in prayer and invo-
cation, they were approached by an officious French
officer who attempted to restrain them on the grounds
that the British might hear. The Odawas replied that
Manitou would prevent their words from reaching the
enemy, and were henceforth left in peace.[33]

The advance party was in sight of Fort William Henry on the
morning of August 3, after threading its way in medieval grandeur
through the beautiful island archipelagoes of the lake, the huge
main body following behind in a celebratory mood. That mood
was perhaps justified, as the English defenders of Fort William
Henry looked north to view with dismay the 250 French *bateaux*
and 150 great canoes which formed merely the head of the column.
A number of the *bateaux* had been joined together, with platforms
between the hulls, to carry field guns. The worried British commandant, Lieutenant Colonel George Monro — "an old officer but
who had never served in the Field" — sent off several appeals for
help to Fort Edward on the Hudson, observing ominously that "we
know that they have Cannon."[34]

If Monro and his British garrison had any doubts as to what fate
potentially awaited them, it had been graphically demonstrated a few
weeks earlier when a party of New Jersey men, exploring in twenty-two
boats north on Lake George under the command of Colonel John
Parker, was ambushed by a body of warriors who had ranged south
from Carillon. Bougainville relates what took place:

> At daybreak, three of these barges fell into our ambush
> and surrendered without a shot fired. Three others
> that followed at a little distance met the same fate....
> The Indians who were on the shore fired at [the
> remainder] and made them fall back. When they saw
> them do this they jumped into their canoes ... and
> sank or captured all but two who escaped. They
> brought back nearly two hundred prisoners. The rum
> which was in the barges and which the Indians imme-

diately drank caused them to commit great cruelties.
They put in the pot and ate three prisoners.[35]

The question of European alcohol and its power to distort warrior behaviour beyond the comprehension of the Europeans was
returned to, perceptively, by Bougainville throughout his journal. It
remains, however, an underexamined aspect of the war; if the warriors fought their enemies on an entirely different ethical basis than
the French their primary purpose remained the obtaining of status
and prestige through "distinguishing ourselves, and of getting some
prisoners and scalps to show our people that we had been at war."[36]
Within that framework, the warriors of the Iroquois and allied
nations pursued an honourable method of warfare by their own
lights, which included the killing of unprofitable prisoners and the
taking of plunder as a matter of course. The practice of cannibalism
was by no means universal, and further confusion would arise with
the warrior propensity to refer to prisoners as "meat," even if there
were no culinary intentions. The degree to which warrior atrocities
were a product of alcoholic distortion of behaviour rather than of
ingrained traits remains inadequately studied.

It should be noted that to become a prisoner of, for examle,
the Iroquois and be adopted by the nation if not ransomed by the
French, frequently led to voluntary permanent membership and
not necessarily a hell of torture and early death. An Iroquois warrior, Tontileaugo, adopted an English captive with the following
words that reflect very little of mindless savagery and a good deal
of societal wisdom and responsibility; it was in many respects the
capacity of the North American warrior to be at once a noble,
brave and dignified figure and a nightmarish terror in European
eyes that bedevilled those, like the sensitive and observant
Bougainville, who attempted to understand and reconcile these
very different and often conflicting qualities.

You are taken into the Caughnewago [sic] nation, and
initiated into a warlike tribe. You are adopted into a
great family, and now received with great seriousness

58

and solemnity in the room and place of a great man. After what is passed this day, you are now one of us by an old law and custom. My son, you now have nothing to fear; we are now under the same obligations to love, support and defend you, that we are to love and defend one another. Therefore you are to consider yourself as one of our people.[37]

The garrison that Lieutenant Colonel Monro had at his disposal to repel the formidable force approaching him consisted of five companies of the 35th Regiment of Foot and additional companies of New York and New Jersey provincial troops. Shortly before the arrival of Montcalm's leading warriors, General Webb, twenty miles away to the south at the British post of Fort Edward, had sent off two hundred men of the 60th Foot (Royal Americans) and eight hundred Massachusetts provincial troops, under Lieutenant Colonel Joseph Frye, to reinforce Monro — although he would send no more, despite repeated entreaties from Monro. These troops arrived scant hours before Montcalm began his assault, to join the ailing garrison and the few sailors, workmen, women and children who were with them. Smallpox was spreading through the garrison, and as the French assault began to unfold, Monro had barely more than a thousand men able to stand to their posts.[38]

The fortification these ailing men were preparing to defend was a four-pointed redoubt of logs built at the southern end of Lake George, immediately to the west of a creek that ran into the lake through swampy land. On the east side of the creek, atop a low rise, the British had also built a palisaded camp, or "retrenchment." On arrival at William Henry, Montcalm sent the advance guard and the warriors around to the south of the fort and the "retrenchment" to block any movement along the road southward to Fort Edward. Meanwhile, the regular troops approached along the western side of the lake, preparing for a formal European-style siege. As decorum dictated, Montcalm sent in a flag of truce to Monro, calling for the garrison's surrender. Montcalm raised the spectre of warrior slaughter.

[H]umanity obliged him to warn [Monro] that once [the French] batteries were in place and the cannon fired, perhaps there would not be time, nor would it be in [his] power, to restrain the cruelties of a mob of Indians of so many different nations.[39]

Monro was unmoved, replying that he would resist "to the last extremity," and while the warriors swarmed round the edges of the scene, the industrious, antlike French set to work with their pickaxes and shovels. For Monro, it became evident within one day that the French would bring artillery to bear which his log and gravel ramparts would not withstand. By August 8, the relentless bombardment the French had opened had rained down on the fort and the fortified camp had inflicted such casualties and damage in both places that Monro called a council of war of his officers, who urged him to make terms with Montcalm. A drummer and flag of truce appeared on the ramparts, and negotiations for the surrender of Monro's garrison began. Colonel Young of the William Henry garrison came out and met Bougainville, who was charged by Montcalm to draw up the terms and negotiate them with the English.

Montcalm was true to his professional ethics, and Monro found himself and his garrison granted terms on the most honourable basis, a compliment to his courage in resisting the assault. In return for undertaking to be "paroled" into noncombatant status for eighteen months, the garrison was to be allowed to march out with arms and personal effects, colours and a field piece, and to be escorted by the French to Fort Edward. The military stores in the fort would be left to the French, and all English wounded and sick would be cared for by the French and returned when well. This agreement, exemplary of European civility in war, was arrived at by Montcalm with no prior consultation with his warrior allies, and flew in the face of the warriors' expectations regarding prisoners, trophies and valuable plunder such as weapons. When the warriors learned of this agreement, their sense of betrayal after having flocked to the French banner turned to a determination to take what they felt was theirs and decamp. On August 10, as the column of English began to depart for Fort Edward, the warriors broke into English stocks of rum and brandy and soon fell on the formation in a wild melee of slaughter and plunder that the French tried, and failed, to prevent. By the day's end, just under two hundred regular and provincial soldiers, and families who had followed them, had been killed, including all wounded and sick in French care. More than twice as many had been seized as prisoners and were being stripped and marched north and west by their captors, for ransom or adoption if they survived the march. Perhaps five hundred found safety with the French escort force, and the remainder found an unknown fate in the gloom of the forest, straggling in to Fort Edward for days thereafter.

For Bougainville, sent away to Montreal with news of the victory before the massacre, and who had warned the English what to expect from the warriors ("I had taken care upon going into the English camp to advise the officers and soldiers to throw away all wine, brandy and intoxicating liquors; they themselves realized of what consequence it was for them to take this precaution"[40]) the turn of events was a humiliating and bitter shock. To him, Montcalm had done all that could have been expected to avoid such a catastrophe.

> Before signing the capitulation, the Marquis de Montcalm assembled a council to which the chiefs of all the nations had been summoned. He informed them of the articles granted the besieged, the motives which determined his according them, asked their consent and their promise that their young men would not commit any disorder. The chiefs agreed to everything and promised to restrain their young men. One sees by this action of the Marquis de Montcalm to what point one is a slave to the Indians in this country. They are a necessary evil.[41]

The essential gulf in understanding between Montcalm and his European, professional sensibilities and the entirely different ethos of the warriors could not have been more starkly illuminated by this event. The dismay of the warriors — regardless of chiefly assertions — caused them to fade from this moment onward as the vital ally of the French; after William Henry, never again would such numbers of warriors come to serve Onontio. For Montcalm, as likely for the ambivalent Bougainville, this brought relief — now war could be fought as European professionals would fight it — but it came with a fatal price. As historian Fred Anderson has pointed out, the aftermath of Fort William Henry put an end to Vaudreuil's carefully crafted Indian alliance system while hardening British instincts toward vengeance rather than civility; it also brought to the warriors an unexpected calamity.

> The western Indians would discover too late that the English and Provincials at William Henry had been suffering from smallpox, and thus that the captives, scalps and clothing they brought back carried the seeds of a great epidemic which would devastate their homelands. No warriors from the *pays d'en haut* would help Montcalm again, and even the converts from the St. Lawrence missions would become reluctant to take up the hatchet.... Although the conflict [was] Europeanized after 1757, British officers would never be inclined to offer the honours of war to any French force. At the same time, provincial outrage over "the massacre of Fort William Henry" would feed an already ferocious anti-Catholic tradition in New England and intensify an undiscriminating Anglo-American hatred of Indians.[42]

That Montcalm's policy cost the French the one weapon, beyond their own courage, which might have secured for them a victory in North America may not have been lost at some level on Bougainville, but his capacity for sympathy toward the warrior approach to war, and his intimate experience of Indian life that included Ceuta's loving embrace, was nonetheless shattered against the wall of gratuitous cruelty the warriors erected before his eyes. It was too much to forgive or understand.

The Indians arrived at Montreal in a crowd with about two hundred English [prisoners from William Henry].... They did not spare the Brandy, and this liquor, the god of the Indians, abounds in their camp. They get drunk, and the English die a hundred deaths from fear every day. At two o'clock, in the presence of the entire town, they killed one of them, put him in a kettle, and forced his unfortunate companions to eat him.... That is enough of the horror, the memory of which I would hope could be effaced from the minds of men. *Heu fuge crudeles terras fuge littus iniquum!* [Ah! Flee the cruel lands, flee the cruel shore!][43]

In the month following the events on Lake George, Bougainville busied himself with writing Montcalm's official report to the various ministries that required them — Vaudreuil would send his own, telling a very different story — while the governor slowly ransomed the surviving English prisoners still in the possession of warriors encamped outside Montreal. Ahead of Bougainville lay a winter of coping with the evils of the colonial administration, burying himself in Ceuta's arms, and preparing for the campaign of 1758. As the gloom of November and then the first snows fell, it was evident that Bougainville was developing a healthy loathing of the iniquities of the Colony.

M. de Bellestre's detachment has returned after having destroyed the Palatine village on the Mohawk River. The Indians pillaged and burned everything. They brought back much plunder and 150 prisoners, among whom was the mayor of the village. We had only three men lightly wounded. The Acadians [who were refugees from the expulsion of 1755] die in crowds. Their past and present misery, the greed of the Canadians, who only try to squeeze out of them all the money they can, and then refuse them the goods so dearly bought, are the cause of this mortality.[44]

With the coming of spring in 1758, Bougainville found himself involved in the planning of a powerful and destructive sweep through New York which was to be led by the highly capable François-Gaston, duc de Lévis, Montcalm's second in command. The force was to be composed of a thousand warriors from the Christianized "seven towns" Iroquois of the St. Lawrence Valley and fifteen hundred French regular troops, with some Canadian militia. The plan was a bold one: landing from Lake Ontario at Oswego, striking up the Oswego River to the portage that connected to the Mohawk River, then sweeping eastward along the Mohawk Valley in a raid of plunder and destruction that was designed to impress anglophilic Mohawk warriors with resurgent French power and to divert British attention from the Lake Champlain corridor. The force had been assembled and got under way, but before it reached the open waters of Lake Ontario, word came that a powerful British army was moving up the Hudson–Lake George corridor toward Carillon.[45]

If the gulf in comprehension that irrevocably split apart the French fighting formula at Fort William Henry signalled the beginning of the end for French fortunes in America, the rise to power of William Pitt in Great Britain, and his personal assumption of the conduct of the war, comprised no less ominous a sign. Lord Loudon had been relieved, new commanders appointed and a grand and cohesive strategy for the conquest of New France embarked upon, one that called for a methodical advance on all fronts — the Niagara frontier, the Oswego–Cataraqui route and down the St. Lawrence, the Lake Champlain corridor, and the ascent to Quebec via Louisbourg — supported by increasing British mastery of the sea and effective financing of the war's costs. As Montcalm moved south now to take personal command of the defence of Carillon, and Bougainville went with him, the vast army toiling north toward Carillon under Major General James Abercromby was the first tentacle of this reborn octopus of British power, uncoiling fatefully northward.

Word had arrived at Montreal of the approach of Abercromby's army on June 29, and by July 8, when the clash was to come, only the European troops, some Canadian colony troops and Canadian militia had arrived to bolster Carillon's garrison. It would be almost entirely a European struggle, and it was fought with that mixture of resolute bravery, appalling slaughter and blinkered leadership that remained forever as incomprehensible to the casualty-wary warriors as their own assumptions about prisoners, torture, and the true aims of war were to the Europeans.

The fortification at Carillon/Ticonderoga — in the present day rebuilt to an approximation of its appearance in 1758 — sits on a low bluff of land at the southern end of Lake Champlain, where the lake narrows and divides into the creek that flows from Lake George, and the southward-continuing arm of the lake known as Wood Creek. It is beautifully sited to enjoy a southern exposure, but inefficient in a military sense, as it is dominated by a height of land to the southwest — later known as Mount Defiance — while to the northwest, there is high ground on the landward approaches to the fort. It was on this latter high ground that Montcalm sensibly decided to throw out a semicircular defensive work of tangled tree stumps and branches, an *abatis*, before which was left a rough, stump-dotted clearing that afforded a clear field of fire to the French defenders sheltering behind the *abatis*. To defend this outwork and the fort itself, Montcalm would have at his eventual disposal some three thousand French regular troops, four hundred colony troops, a party of Canadian militia and a handful of loyal warriors. Toiling north toward them was an awesome body of some fifteen thousand British regular troops and provincials, whose pace was such that the *abatis* might not be completed before they arrived.

For Bougainville, who had endured a spring amidst an exhausted and hungry population — the previous harvest had failed — and the endless cycle of bickering, overt profiteering, public misery and jockeying for power between Montcalm and Vaudreuil, the orders that sent him southward with Montcalm on June 24, even before Abercromby's march had been reported, were a welcome escape. Travelling slowly southward by a mixture of horseback and *bateaux* on the Richelieu River, he learned, while paused at Saint-Jean, that the fortress of Louisbourg had been attacked and a landing secured by the British. Bougainville was both angry and cynical after reading the accounts.

But why did not the troops charged with defending
the works at [the landing beaches], after the first
artillery and musket fire, charge the English with the
bayonet and overwhelm them? Why did not the other
nearby troops also charge? The bad feelings between
the two corps, and the greed of M. Prévost, who con-
trols M. de Drucour, will make the King lose
Louisbourg.[46]

On arrival at Carillon, Bougainville found also, by a dispatch
which caught up with him, that he had received a promotion, courtesy
of the king, to a more senior status than that of simply an aide: *aide-
maréchal des logis*, essentially a senior quartermaster.

The news of the advance of Abercromby's huge force from the
south sent a wave of panic through the Carillon garrison, aware that
unless something slowed the English advance the fort would not be
prepared to resist its attack. A chance encounter between Abercromby's
advance troops and a French scouting party provided that needed
pause. A casualty of the skirmish turned out to be the ablest officer in
Abercromby's leadership: Brigadier George Augustus, Viscount Howe,
a skilled and beloved light infantryman. Bougainville recorded the
event with professional respect:

The enemy suffered a considerable loss there in the
person of Milord Howe, who was killed. He was [a]
brigadier general and had showed the greatest talents,
although still in his youth. He had above all in the
greatest degree those two qualities of heros, activity
and audacity. He it was who had projected the enterprise against Canada, and he alone was capable of exe-
cuting it.... His death stopped the advance. The disheartened English gave us twenty-four hours' delay,
and this precious time was the saving of us and the
colony ... most glorious for him is the respect of his
compatriots and the esteem of the French.[47]

While Howe had lived, there had been a spirit and purpose to the army. With his death, initiative seemed to evaporate, and the over-weight, indecisive Abercromby — nicknamed "Granny" by his troops — dithered as to what to do next. When he did act, it was to play directly into Montcalm's hands.

The halt of the British had allowed, as Bougainville noted, Montcalm to push every member of the garrison, officer and enlisted man alike, into finishing in a ten-hour effort the defensive works on the higher ground northwest of the fort. When Abercromby finally shifted from his torpor, it was not to see if artillery emplacements could be set up — on Mount Defiance, for example — to batter Carillon into submission, but to send forward a single engineer officer to look briefly at Montcalm's works and report back. The engineer, a "very junior lieutenant" in Anderson's words[48,] made only a cursory examination of the strong French position, looked for no flanking possibilities, and stated to "Granny" that the place could be taken by a frontal assault. Without soliciting second opinions from his senior officers or looking at the place himself, Abercromby ordered his army to simply array itself in three lines — eight regular battalions in the front, supported by the reserve of six provincial regiments — and undertake a face-on, frontal assault of the *abatis*. Shortly after noon on July 8, 1758, the lines of red-coated infantry marched forward.

For Bougainville, stationed behind the *abatis* near Montcalm in the centre of the French line, the battle was a smoke-filled, seven-hour scene of carnage in which the British formations, tangled and thrown out of alignment by the *abatis*, struggled again and again through the entanglements toward the final French breastworks, only to be cut down by an almost continuous hail of shot. Bougainville's personal role in the fight is not known, but it would have been customary for him to have carried a light officer's musket and to have used it. He remained in the thick of the struggle and was briefly felled by a glancing wound to the head. The struggle ended, unbelievably, with a withdrawal from the field by the British that turned into a panicked near-rout.

> [B]y dawn on July 9, the largest English army ever
> assembled in America was rowing for its life up

Lake George, fleeing an enemy not a quarter of its size — and not in pursuit. By sunset the ruin of Abercrombly's [sic] army collapsed, exhausted, beside the hulk of Fort William Henry. That Abercrombly had crowned defeat with humiliation was apparent to everyone.[49]

For Bougainville, the euphoria of the battle's success was sobered by the reality that the fleeing army was largely intact and its northward return was only a matter of time. The bickering between Montcalm and Vaudreuil was now going to approach visceral enmity, as Vaudreuil sought to discount Montcalm's success. And there were signs that the crop failure that had produced near famine conditions the winter before was about to repeat itself. Over the remainder of the summer, Bougainville divided his time between the strengthening of Carillon's defences and the undertaking of arduous reconnaissance patrols with warriors and militiamen to the south, clad again in the garb of *la petite guerre.* More formally, he was sent under a flag of truce directly to Abercromby's camp to negotiate prisoner exchanges, where he was treated with great civility by the British officers. Back in Carillon, he fruitlessly composed proposal after proposal for daring attacks against British posts, even proposing himself to the minister of marine, through his *chère maman,* Madame Hérault de Séchelles, as leader of a seaborne raid against the British Hudson's Bay Company posts, in the manner of Iberville sixty years earlier. Closer to home, Bougainville perceived that neither the French nor the British seemed to have realized the impact that inland naval power might have on the struggles in North America, and in this he was correct, observing just after Montcalm had won his victory:

> If we wish to avoid the loss of the colony which, this time again, was saved only by a miracle (and one will always be necessary to save it in the state it always is in whenever attacked) the only way to assume ourselves the possession of Lake Champlain and St. Frédéric River is by a strong naval force. I hear of chebecs, half

68

galleys, *bateaux*... of officers and experienced crews. Then all portaging of barges will be useless for the English: they are destroyed as soon as they appear.[50]

In his private letters home to Madame Hérault de Séchelles, Bougainville reveals far more of his misgivings and his deep dismay at the endless bickering and corruption in the colonial administration. Now the equally endless tedium of waiting for the English to mount a serious challenge — fatal though he knew it would be — began to tell on him, and he began to express to *chère maman* his deep wish to come home, writing in one letter, "[T]here is nothing to learn here. You cannot even test yourself and know if you are brave. The English are not defending themselves, and half the year is spent in idleness."[51]

His wishes were about to be fulfilled. As early as the summer of Fort William Henry, Madame Hérault had begun the process of extracting her adoptive son out of the wilderness of Canada and returning him to France. Now her efforts were to bear fruit.

> [B]y now Catherine Hérault was an even greater source of influence: her son-in-law, Peyrenc de Moras, was now Minister of Marine. In late 1757, all the necessary correspondence relating to Bougainville's return was initiated. Montcalm wanted Bougainville to go in order to explain to Versailles the true state of affairs in the colony.... Vaudreuil would have to approve Bougainville's leaving, not a likely prospect since the French military men and the Governor disliked each other intensely. Vaudreuil could not, however, refuse a request from Minister Moras.[52]

By September of 1758, Bougainville received the welcome news he wanted. His journal is strangely very correct on the matter, knowing as he did that Vaudreuil mistrusted him, believing he would distort his story to favour Vaudreuil's hated rival Montcalm, and was only agreeing to the travel because of Moras's pressure.

The Marquis de V., appreciating the critical position of the colony, is determined to send to France an officer to render an account to the court of the end of the campaign. He has condescended to choose me for this important and delicate commission. I would only congratulate myself if I felt I had as much talent to execute it well as I have zeal and good will.[53]

Vaudreuil was true to his nature, and for Bougainville's eyes wrote the following as part of the open letter of recommendation Bougainville was to hand the court:

The state of affairs in the colony, seeming to me to require that I should send a competent officer capable of giving an adequate account of the circumstances, I have chosen, in conjunction with M. the Marquis de Montcalm, M. de Bougainville, Assistant-Quartermaster of this army.... No one is better equipped than he to fulfill this mission.[54]

To Berryer, the new minister of marine, Vaudreuil wrote secretly:

I have granted letters of recommendation to M. Doreil and M. Bougainville; but I reserve to myself the honour of remarking to Your Lordship that these gentlemen are not possessed of a sufficiently intimate knowledge of the colony and its real interests to entitle them to the privilege of discussing the subject with you.... I should warn Your Lordship that these gentlemen, being the creatures of M. de Montcalm, are in complete agreement with his views, and I have little doubt they will endeavour to suppress, or at least belittle, the part played by the colony, and so to claim for the troops in the field the credit for every advantage we have gained over the enemy.[55]

Thus empowered and undermined, Bougainville returned to Montreal, where he put his affairs in order, bid farewell to his Turtle Clan native family and Ceuta, and left for France. The first part of the trip was in an open *bateau* under oar and sail which was carrying five English officers as prisoners to Quebec. Leaving Montreal on November 3, 1758, the boat foundered in the river twenty-six miles above Quebec, and Bougainville and his companions passed a miserable night on a rock in the river a bare six feet above the storm-driven waves. When the morning light revealed that the boat had been battered beyond repair by the storm, Bougainville and the others were forced to swim and wade over two miles in freezing conditions to reach the shore and shelter, an achievement that spoke well of his general hardiness and fitness. Bougainville was unimpressed: "What a country! What a journey! Better be a civilian than have to suffer this sort of thing!" he later grumped in his journal.[56]

Once at Quebec, Bougainville was given passage in the *Victoire*, an eighteen-gun privateer vessel from St-Malo that was under contract to the king. Sailing at midnight on November 11, the *Victoire*'s voyage proved to be a fifty-two-day ordeal of storms, misery, cold, threatened shipwreck and misnavigation. The ship was twice on the brink of foundering, leading the terrified crew to vow that "wherever the ship should first touch land they would have a solemn mass celebrated, to which they swore to walk in procession clad only in their shirts, and barefoot."[57]

By November 30, the hapless ship and its wretched people were approaching the end of their endurance, and Bougainville no less so:

> November 29–30. Southeast winds prevailed, great tempest with squalls. Frightful night, fearful rolling, no [safe] position to take, the blows of the sea wet down every part of the ship.... Oh, three and four times happier the gardener who plants cabbages, for he always has one foot on the ground and the other is only away from it the length of the shovel.... Oh, God! The sea has no end for us, even its shores are missing.[58]

As his biographer Thiéry drily points out, "the passion for seamanship which was afterward to take possession of Bougainville showed no sign of its existence during this frightful voyage: actually, it inspired lines scarcely worthy of a son of Neptune."[59]

This litany of endurance came to a climax when, through poor navigation and a possibly faulty compass, the leaking, battered *Victoire* almost wrecked itself in the Bristol Channel rather than approaching Belle Isle, on the French coast, where they believed themselves to be. Sheepishly asking help from fishermen and dodging English cruisers, *Victoire* managed at last to blunder into landfall on the French coast, and by December 20 Bougainville was safe in the arms of his *chère maman* and breathing, as Thiéry puts it, "the intoxicating air of Paris."[60] Ahead lay the intrigues of Versailles and a return again to North America. But for the moment the moccasin trails, the bloodied scalping knife and the horrors of the distant war were behind him, and he was home.

Chapter Four

The Final Days and Canada's Surrender, 1759–1760

Very soon after disembarking at Morlaix and making his way to Paris, Bougainville was forced to tear himself way from the warmth and comfort of the Hérault de Séchelles home and get on with his task, which was, as Vaudreuil had ordered, to report to the various ministries and the court itself on the situation in the colony, hopefully in pursuit of more men and supplies for its defence. In particular, Vaudreuil had instructed Bougainville to report that if any extraordinary expenditures had occurred in the colony's accounting, they had been entirely the fault of the *intendant*, Bigot, and not Vaudreuil. With this bit of political blame-shifting and the more alarming news of the state of Canada's defences, Bougainville sought out the appropriate government ministers.

His first call was on the new minister of marine, Nicolas René Berryer, who had replaced Peyrenc de Moras, *chère maman*'s son-in-law. Bougainville outlined to a very preoccupied Berryer the reality that, with the spring, the British forces would be in a position to muster against Canada a body of some 80,000 men under arms, backed by an increasing mastery of the sea. To face this enemy, the French in Canada could present just over 3,000 regular metropolitan troops, 1,200 colony soldiers of the *Compagnies franches de la Marine* and some 6,000 militia in varying degrees of readiness. French supplies were so depleted that the rampart ordnance at Quebec had an ammunition supply that would last no more than a

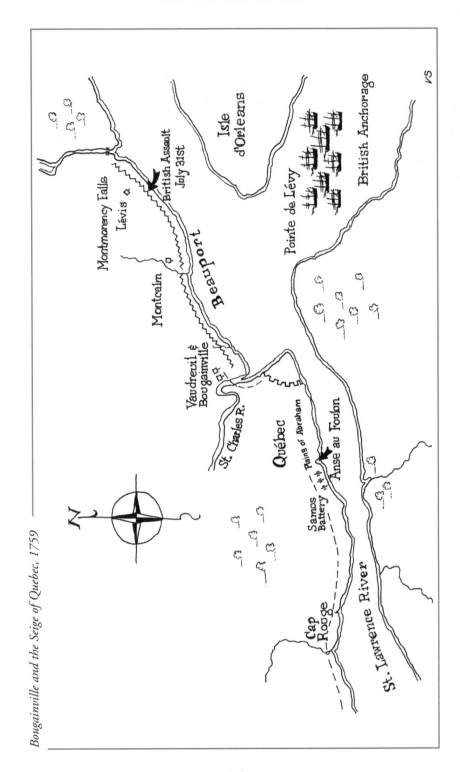

Bougainville and the Seige of Quebec, 1759

week if an attack came, and starvation stalked the population through a lack of flour and virtually every other provision.[1]

Berryer, who was very new to his duties, was intent on French fortunes on the continent, and displayed to Bougainville little enthusiasm for the plea for more troops, supplies and naval support. The French navy had begun a precipitous decline in strength and quality, which Berryer seemed not to understand. What *was* clear to him was the low interest he had in the fortunes of a distant, expensive and undervalued colony. In response to Bougainville's requests, he uttered the observation that "...one doesn't try to save the stables when the house is on fire," to which the disappointed Bougainville lamely replied, "At least, monsieur, no one will be able to say you speak like a horse."[2]

Bougainville fared no better with his presentations to the foreign minister, the Duc de Choiseul, who was equally new to his tasks and unwilling to commit anything like the resources Bougainville stated were needed in Canada. Both ministers listened to a greater degree to Bougainville's candid observations that the rivalry between Vaudreuil and Montcalm were poisonous to the health of the colony. Berryer sent Vaudreuil a thinly veiled instruction to remove himself from the military affairs of the colony except *in extremis*:

> It remains to me to impress upon you the importance of remaining in perfect agreement with M. de Montcalm and of forgetting the petty differences of opinion which may have formerly existed between you.... You yourself should not take part in any campaign unless it be of a nature so decisive that you find yourself obliged, for the general defence of the colony, to place in action all the militia of the country. Short of a crisis of this gravity, you should remain at the administrative centre of the colony, and so be in a position to keep watch on all that passes.[3]

The new minister of war, Belle-Isle, was no more receptive to Bougainville's pleas, and in response sent a letter to Montcalm informing him the court was contemplating a major military effort in Europe and the requested help could not be forthcoming. He offered to provide up to four hundred recruits for the regular regiments, some sixty artillerymen, engineers and fortification specialists, and some powder and provisions. Bougainville was aghast at the paltry support, but Montcalm would eventually write back to Berryer, "To him who has nothing, even a little counts." The bottom line was that Paris could not — or would not — act to save the colony, and its fate was virtually sealed.

Bougainville refused to admit defeat, however. Through family connections, he managed, after much cooling of his heels in Versailles antechambers and false alarms, to secure an interview with the king's mistress and de facto policy advisor, Madame de Pompadour. She was a beautiful, intelligent and utterly unprincipled woman, and while the depth of their relationship is not a matter of record, Pompadour was clearly impressed with this articulate, charming and warmly passionate young officer who had about him, beneath the powder, lace and brocade of a gentleman, the hard, muscled physicality of a North American forest warrior. Whether that stirred her to a relationship more intimate and personal than the simple extension of her enthusiastic support is unknown, but Bougainville found that she offered all her influence on his behalf as he voiced a daring — and largely impractical — scheme to reduce the pressure on the besieged colony.

Bougainville argued for a diversionary assault landing by a French force of four thousand on the beaches of the Carolinas. This body would then march north and split the newly developing focus of the Thirteen Colonies on the destruction of New France. Bougainville reasoned that the German settlers in America — whom he claimed "the English treat like slaves in their colonies" — and the Cherokee tribes would rise in common hatred of the British Crown and welcome the French, and that this rising would not be opposed by the pacifist Quaker population. It was a concept eerily prescient of what would take place twenty-two years later in

America, but in 1759 Bougainville was making an astonishingly naïve proposal:

> Bougainville misread the discontent, for few of the American colonists would have allied themselves with a Catholic absolutist regime in spite of the complaints they had against King and Parliament. Yet Bougainville blithely concluded his memorandum to the king's mistress by stating that if the French were not successful in their invasion sweep from Carolina to Canada, they could always retreat to Louisiana where food supplies would have been stocked in anticipation of potential failure.[4]

Madame de Pompadour's energetic championing of Bougainville also afforded him opportunities to defend Montcalm's reputation against the secret representations Vaudreuil had sent by another courier, but Bougainville was aghast at the precarious state of France and the uncertainties caused by rapidly changing ministerial appointments, a weak king dominated by his willful mistress — not that Bougainville could personally complain of that fact — and an empty treasury. He wrote secretly to Montcalm: "Wherever you look, a lack of stability, both in the council chamber and in the public forum. Credit, none. In the Exchequer everything left to chance.... In short, if you do not lose all, you will gain a triumph."[5]

> The king greeted Bougainville warmly, several audiences being granted due in large part to Pompadour's insistence, but it came as no surprise to Bougainville that his proposals for the attack on the Carolinas, and his main request for support for New France, were politely shrugged away. Honours and awards flowed, where actual support did not, however: two years before being normally eligible for the honour, Bougainville found himself made a

full colonel and awarded, along with Bourlamaque, the cross of a Chevalier de Saint-Louis. He was to carry back the king's appointment of Montcalm to the rank of lieutenant-general, and Lévis to major-general. Vaudreuil, the bitter adversary, was advanced with the granting of the Grand Cross of Saint-Louis as a kind of solace for having been chastised over his squabbles with Montcalm. It was a bestowing of ribbons and honours, because the true support needed was either unavailable, or not of concern to a disinterested court, however much *La Pompadour*'s delicately powdered bosom palpitated to Bougainville's combination of charm, optimism and manly virtue.

Thiéry paints the scene clearly: France, exhausted as she was by the European war, miscalculated the importance attached to the retention of the precious colony, and watched the unfolding of the great drama in America with complete indifference. Voltaire wondered why they wasted their time quarrelling with England over "a few acres of snow," and the former Secretary of State for War, the Comte d'Argenson, declared that he would give away all of France's colonies in India and America for a pin's head. And yet, in nine years France had spent in Canada more than a hundred million livres — a heavy load for the people to bear — while England for her part was about to stake two milliards on the other side of the Atlantic so that she might wrest from France her finest colony.[6]

In France's defence, the fall of Louisbourg in midsummer 1758 and the loss of French slaving posts on the Senegal that same year had galvanized Prime Minister William Pitt, who saw that the long and protracted land war in Europe was far from the goal of beating an exhausted but still formidable France to its knees. He would press on with a relentless campaign to destroy France in its colonial possessions, and was aided in planning this scheme by two officers of extraordinary capability: the First Lord of the Admiralty, Lord Anson, and the commander-in-chief of the army, Lord Ligonier. The cooperative excellence of this triumvirate, and the solid financial mechanisms of the British administration, meant that in the global sweep of the great struggle, Bougainville's little prize of attractive ribbons and four hundred raw recruits was essentially meaningless.[7]

If the contest for Canada was now merely a matter of the inevitable, there was still duty to be done. Bougainville morosely surveyed his two months of pleading and polite conversation and packed up to return to the doomed colony. If the king was entrusting everything "to Montcalm's zeal and generalship, joined with the valour of the victors of Ticonderoga," there was little to hope for except personal honour and the faint possibility of unlikely miracles. With a tearful embrace from his *chère maman* and a last visit to Madame de Pompadour — whether her salon or her boudoir — Bougainville journeyed through the bleak February landscape to Bordeaux, and there went aboard the small frigate *La Chézine*, which was to sail as part of a supply convoy destined for the overseas colonies, some of the vessels meant for Quebec. At the end of February 1759, the squadron beat its way out into the bitter North Atlantic on a passage that would take the Quebec-bound vessels two months because of the winds, but which would pass without the terrifying experiences of his last time at sea. Bougainville had nothing negative to say about the experience, and perhaps he was coming to feel the first inklings of the attraction of the naval life, rather than its horrors.[8]

As *La Chézine* approached the Canadian coastline, however, perils other than misnavigation or midwinter gales lay in wait. The British had assembled a powerful naval expeditionary force under Vice Admiral Charles Saunders that had sailed for North America in mid February, bearing the army of the tubercular and deathly seasick James Wolfe, who had been brevetted a major general and was intent on an ascent of the St. Lawrence and the capture of Quebec. Both Saunders' huge fleet — twenty-two ships of the line and more than eighty transports and smaller vessels — and Bougainville's clutch of Quebec-bound ships arrived off Canada at roughly the same time, the faster French ships having made better time. On their arrival, both fleets encountered vast stretches of floating pack ice, which lay offshore up to sixty miles; the winter of 1758–59 had been the coldest in living memory. The French were held up for more than a week in the Cabot Strait until a lead through the ice appeared, and with favourable easterly winds they were able to work into the Gulf of St. Lawrence. The same ice providentially prevented them from being intercepted by the Halifax squadron of Rear Admiral Philip Durrell, whose orders had been to patrol aggressively off the mouth of the St. Lawrence as soon in the new season as possible, but who had been trapped in Halifax harbour by the impenetrable ice. Saunders made for Louisbourg, the staging harbour for the Quebec assault, but turned away from that icebound place and managed to get into Halifax. The same breakup of the ice pans allowed Durrell to get his ships out and engage in his St. Lawrence patrol on May 5, 1759, while Saunders' ships paused to recover at Halifax, then moved to Louisbourg to embark more troops and begin the ascent of the river behind Durrell. Durrell's orders had been to proceed up the great river in advance of the main fleet as far as the modern town of Rimouski, and there await Saunders. He pressed his squadron further up the river, however, capturing three small French coasting vessels — and with them the news that a group of French ships had slipped into the river ahead of them and safely reached Quebec. One of those ships was Bougainville's *La Chézine.*[9]

Bougainville, for his part, was exultant, and wrote to Madame Hérault de Séchelles: "The English will never take me now, having missed me this time"![10] His journal entry was more laconic:

> I reached Quebec May 10, after having been for ten
> days in the ice between Cape North and Cape Ray.
> The [rest of the] Bordeaux fleet arrived three days

after me, and on May 23 the advance of the English squadron was at Bic.[11]

Bougainville may have been pleased at his luck in evading capture, but as *La Chézine*'s crew put a tight harbour furl in their topsails below the looming heights of Quebec, the river downstream was witnessing the advance of an ominous armada, an advance as remarkable for the number of ships it involved — some 140 — as for the superb seamanship that was bringing it, hour by hour, closer to the anchorage in the basin before Quebec, on the south side of Île d'Orléans.

The French had removed what buoys there were from the river and relied on a system of local pilots to make the sometimes difficult passage above Île-aux-Coudres to Quebec. The channel lay now to the north side of the river, now to the south. The most trying and risky part of the passage was at the eastern end of Île d'Orléans, where a narrow channel known as the Traverse brought shipping from the north shore in a treacherous diagonal path to the south before entering Quebec's basin; here, the navigable channel was barely as wide as the beam of Saunders' largest ships. The navigation of Saunders' fleet was being guided by the sounding work of the various ships' sailing masters, who went out ahead of the fleet in a flotilla of longboats and used lead and line to feel the way through.

Coordinating their efforts was James Cook, sailing master of the *Pembroke*, armed with sixty-four guns. Cook, a taciturn Yorkshireman, had assembled a composite of captured French charts to aid in the passage up, and had begun to develop a new and radically more advanced charting methodology during the Louisbourg campaign the year before. His expertise, particularly in sounding the Traverse and guiding the ponderous British vessels, one by one, through it, would lead to his eventual fame as a surveyor and chartmaker, and ultimately to command of three Pacific voyages of exploration, the first of which would transit the Pacific Ocean mere months apart from Bougainville. There could be no hint of that relationship, or that their respective writings would impact upon European society with a vision — however unreal — of earthly paradise, on June 27, 1759, when the last of Saunders' fleet, the ninety-gun *Neptune*, came to anchor with the others below Quebec, watched by Montcalm and Bougainville. Montcalm was said to have observed drily, as he witnessed this feat of seamanship, that at least there would now be a good chart of the river.[12]

This vast armament of some 140 ships carried more than 8,000 soldiers, 13,000 seamen and marines, and supporting artillery batteries, along with heavily laden transports. The army's commander, Wolfe, had been selected for his role because of his zeal and energy in the taking of Louisbourg. Ill and intensely disliked by his subordinate brigadiers, Wolfe had to devise a way of taking the formidable prize of Quebec before the coming of winter and the exhaustion of his supplies made it impossible. His first acts were to establish camps on the Île d'Orléans and the south shore; to erect bombardment batteries of artillery on the height of Point Lévis with which to strike at the town; and to begin thinking about where he could conceivably get his superbly trained army ashore and lure Montcalm and his garrison into what Wolfe wanted: a decisive open-field battle that would shorten, or remove entirely, the need for a lengthy and draining siege.

To oppose Wolfe, Montcalm had five French regular battalions and just under 6,000 Canadian colony troops and militia, for a total of some 12,000 of all ranks and functions, if of varying quality. Other forces had been sent to Montreal: one under Bourlamaque to watch the approaches from Lake Champlain, and another, under de la Corne, to monitor the St. Lawrence approaches from Lake Ontario. Bougainville's first duty sent him off to the north shore of the river just below Quebec, at Beauport, to construct defensive positions. "On June 3, I was detached with five companies of grenadiers and five hundred militiamen to build redoubts and lines from the Falls of Montmorency up to Quebec. My camp was enlarged day by day up to the twenty-eighth, as the entire army came to occupy it."[13]

Montcalm considered the long, accessible shoreline below Bougainville's position to be the most likely place where Wolfe would attempt a landing, and in that he was correct. When British advance troops landed on the north shore of the river, just below Montmorency Falls, the signals were plain to the French above that cascade that an attack was imminent. The colony's senior leadership arrived to take command, and Montcalm held the centre, with Lévis on the left, or Montmorency, side of the prepared positions, and Vaudreuil, with Bougainville under him in a diplomatic posting if ever there was one, commanding the right. On July 31, Wolfe did not disappoint Montcalm, launching a major amphibious assault against the Beauport shore and its long slopes leading up to Bougainville's earthworks and firing trenches above. The attack was a disaster for the British: two of the supporting ships were grounded on approach; the longboats carrying in the troops were held up by an unsuspected ledge until a gap through it could be found: and when the infantry managed to wade and stumble ashore, their assault up a long, greasy slope was swept over by a torrential thunderstorm and downpour. The French fired with deadly accuracy from their near-impregnable positions until their own flintlocks began to sputter in the rain, but by then the British attack had broken, and the French did not pursue them as they fell and tumbled down the bloody slope, leaving by Bougainville's estimate six or seven hundred casualties — the British would admit to just over four hundred — and the two grounded ships, burnt to keep them out of French hands. It was a solid victory for the French, and the disposition of the defensive works Bougainville had made.[14]

Montcalm had won the first pass, and the judicious arrangements he had made with his meagre resources — he had left himself an escape route by having the supply ships move upriver some fifty miles to Batiscan, near Trois-Rivières — put the perplexed Wolfe into a difficult situation.

> [T]he defences of Quebec were so nearly seamless that Wolfe could not gain a foothold on the north shore of the St. Lawrence from which he could open a formal siege. So long as the French

remained able to supply themselves, and so long as
Montcalm could shift his forces freely from one
part of the lines to another, Wolfe had little hope
of even beginning a successful siege. To decide the
issue he needed something that had never yet taken
place in America, an open-field battle. Until
Montcalm consented to give him one, he could do
no more than shell the town, ravage the countryside, and issue bombastic proclamations calling for
the French to surrender.[15]

Wolfe sought out, as was the military custom, the advice of his
subordinate brigadiers as to how to crack the nut of Quebec's
defences. Unanimously they recommended that Wolfe look to
secure a landing *above* Quebec, where the lengthy supply lines to
Batiscan and Montreal could be cut and the ground ashore had no
imposing bluffs. Too ill to ignore the advice, and knowing that by
September the chances of securing a victory would indeed diminish
— the navy and its 13,000 sailors could not remain for the winter
— he began to probe for a weak spot upriver from his objective.

It was now that Bougainville entered into a series of actions
which were at once a great credit to him, but in the end were to be
shrouded in some controversy. To counter the possibility that the
British could get a meaningful force above Quebec and establish a
foothold by landing on the more accessible shores there, Montcalm
had posted a number of militia units at key points westward up the
river, but then created a force of what would grow to be 1,000 bet-
ter-quality troops whose task was to move rapidly toward any perceived British landing attempt on the upper river and repulse it.
Command of this mobile force was given to Bougainville, and
action was not long in following.

The brutality with which Wolfe was waging his war against the
canadien population in the countryside around Quebec was lend-
ing a horror to the struggle that put a hard edge to Bougainville.
Word had come of the deliberate ravaging of Quebec settlements,
reminiscent of the slaughter and destruction of the Thirty Years'

War in Europe or the punishment of the Highlands after Culloden in 1746. It was exemplified by an attack on the small village of St-Joachim, west of the Montmorency, by a party of the 43rd Regiment and some American rangers. Its commander, Captain Alexander Montgomery, announced to his men that no prisoners were to be taken. When he arrived at the village, he found the eighty men of the settlement barricaded with the village priest in the latter's house. Confronted with Montgomery's force, the priest thought it prudent to surrender, and even invited Montgomery in for a meal as he and his parishioners left the house. His response was pitiless.

> Captain Montgomery, true to his promise, ordered every man to be shot. Some of them by this time were kneeling in prayer and supplication, but all of them were killed and ... most of them were afterward scalped. The priest himself was slashed to the ground with repeated sword strokes and when lying there he was scalped and his skull smashed.... His parish was burned to the ground. The official reason given for this savage warfare ... was that it would starve Quebec and induce the Canadian militia defending it to desert in order to protect their homes and families.[16]

While the settlements writhed under Wolfe's lash, the Royal Navy was busy providing for his landing attempt upriver. On August 5–6, a small flotilla that included a twenty-two-gun frigate, the *Sutherland,* under Admiral Holmes managed to dash upriver on the flood tide on an easterly wind, having embarked a sizeable force of infantry. Still assembling his command, Bougainville responded to this threat by force-marching the men he did have along the shore road in pursuit of Holmes' ships, following them until they came to anchor off the village of Pointe-aux-Trembles. Two days later, on August 8, the British made their first attempt at an upriver landing. Bougainville recorded the result:

The afternoon of August 8, the enemy anchored broadside before the landing place at Pointe-aux-Trembles a frigate of twenty-two guns and several bomb ships which fired on shore. The landing place was a smooth beach without any covering heights or defenses; I had not had time to make any. Their first landing was made at low tide: their troops, to the number of fifteen hundred men, formed there and marched against me. The cavalry was advanced on my right, and I might have had three hundred men in action. This first attack did not succeed and they re-embarked. My horse was hit. They came on a second time to the attack at high tide and were again pushed back with a loss of three hundred men killed or wounded. On the tenth, the enemy encamped opposite men on the south shore.[17]

Somewhat laconically, Bougainville was documenting that a body of well-trained British infantry had landed on a shore he had had no time to fortify, and that with a force less than a third that of the British he had attacked them frontally, and with the aid of the cavalry detachment beaten off two assault landings, inflicting in the process casualties, if his figures were correct, of between a quarter and a third of the attacking force. It was an astonishing military success, yet the moderate tone of his journal entry is in keeping with Bougainville's nature, for it is visible throughout his writings and his actions that, while he absolutely did not lack for bravery, he could not be described as a true warrior. He did not seem to take the almost sexual delight in the clash of combat and the wounding or killing of others that lies as the heart of those who love war for war's sake and seek it out. He was burdened, perhaps, with his own humanism and intelligent civility, and though he conducted his military duties with honour and an evident sense of loyalty to a gentleman's code, the warmth and optimism which lay at the foundation of his personality were arguably qualities more suited to the embrace of life, rather than its destruction, as a profession. That this reality would possibly lie, at least in part, behind a later decision to abandon an army career in favour of seafaring remains to be demonstrated, but it would affect the remainder of his career in Canada — and possibly alter the history of the continent.

Bougainville's solid defence at Pointe-aux-Trembles sent the British back to an encampment on the far shore, and possibly a decision by Wolfe that he would have to get ashore closer to Quebec and somehow avoid Bougainville's potent little force before it pounced on the landings. Two more such landings were attempted — or feinted — at Deschambault and at St-Augustin, with Bougainville waiting in each case, but Wolfe, without telling his distrustful and despairing brigadiers, had already decided on a landing at another spot. To conceal its intentions, Holmes' little squadron had already begun a maddening pattern of riding upriver on the flood, then falling back down toward Quebec on the ebb, all the while threatening a landing. The gambit forced Bougainville to keep his detachments almost ceaselessly on the march along the vulnerable miles of shoreline. Over a month's endless trudging it gradually turned the competent troops who had won so convincingly at Pointe-aux-Trembles into a shambling, dusty column of men near exhaustion, and none more so than Bougainville, who frequently rode for more than twenty hours a day.

Haggard and worn from the constant strain, Bougainville nonetheless revealed that streak in him that was determined to maintain some semblance of professional dignity and civility in his dealings with his enemy; the way of the brutal Captain Montgomery was not to be his way.

> He ... wrote to officers in the British camp[s], gentlemen with whom he had made friends while he was employed as secretary to de Mirepoix in London. He kept up a regular correspondence with Captain Abercromby, with whom ... he had made and lost the bet of a case of champagne over the taking of Louisbourg [and] sent him French wine in exchange for Bristol beer. "It is necessary

in this barbarous country," he wrote, " to show as
much politeness and humanity as possible, even to
those with whom we are at war." He even kept up
a cordial relationship with General Townsend [one
of Wolfe's brigadiers]...[18]

After the repulse of the British at Deschambault, Bougainville
established a headquarters at Cap Rouge, the upper limit of Holmes'
apparent pattern of river ascents. Montcalm calculated that Wolfe
was being counselled by his brigadiers that, failures so far or not, the
upper river at Cap Rouge, Pointe-aux-Trembles or somewhere else
nearby remained the most practical landing locales. (This was
indeed the case.) Bougainville was sent additional troops, and his
footsore column grew to three thousand men.[19]

To this point, Bougainville had done his duty solidly and well.
His defensive dispositions at Beauport had helped Montcalm repel
the landing attempt there, and with some gallantry Bougainville
had fought off three real or apparent attacks upriver. But as
September began to turn the forests to red and gold, Wolfe mounted
his most serious effort, and it would penetrate the upriver defences
that Bougainville had maintained with such efficiency.

Without telling his fuming brigadiers, Wolfe had decided to
attempt a landing at a small cove just west of Quebec, from which
a steep path ascended to cultivated fields on the heights. How he
decided upon this cove, known as the Anse au Foulon, is unknown,
but at least one historian has suggested that it was pointed out to
him by a Major Robert Stobo, who had recently rejoined Wolfe's
army after a long sojourn as a lightly-guarded prisoner in Quebec
and a daring voyage of escape down the river. To ensure no break in
the pattern of movement which the French had observed so far,
Holmes' upriver squadron, now with added transports that had
squeezed through the Narrows under French guns, rode up on the
flood again as far as Cap Rouge, and anchored there. But now more
than 3,000 infantry were embarked in those ships, and boats and
landing barges clustered close around them. On the night of
September 12, Wolfe made his move.[20]

Wolfe's brigadiers were to remain unaware of where the landing would be attempted this time until late in the evening, a half-hour before the troops were to descend into the boats; only then did Wolfe inform them that the destination was "the *Foulon* distant Upon 2 miles, or 2 ½ from Quebec, where you remember an encampment of 12 or 13 tents, & an abbatis, below it." The encampment at the top of the steep slope was that established by Bougainville to cover the path and an artillery position, the Samos battery, immediately to its west. The detachment was commanded by a Captain de Vergor. But now came into play a series of coincidences and remarkable good fortune — and possibly the distraction of Bougainville's attention — that allowed Wolfe to get ashore.[21]

Earlier that morning of September 12, a contractor named Cadet had sought Bougainville's permission to send down the river that night, from Batiscan to Quebec, a convoy of flour-laden boats. Bougainville had given orders to the standing posts along the stretch from Cap Rouge to Quebec — including Vergor's — to allow the boats to pass in the darkness. But Cadet had then postponed the shipment at the last moment, and word of this did not reach Bougainville or his staff. There had been movement in the darkness on the river, but there was no means for the French to know that it was British movement, and not their own.[22]

At Cap Rouge, Bougainville might have been in position, if he had been vigilant, to notice something extraordinary happening in Holmes' squadron in the river off his headquarters. Two lanterns had been hoisted into the topmasts of Holmes' *Sutherland*, and even though it remained at anchor there, its attendant transports and their accompanying boats began to slip away, one by one, downriver into the gloom. But Bougainville did not perceive these things — possibly because he may not have been there, but at Jacques-Cartier, nine miles away.

> The evening before, Madame de Vienne, the wife of one of Bigot's subordinates whose house outside Quebec Vaudreuil was using as his headquarters, was advised to leave for Montreal. She was an attractive woman whose favours were apparently as much in

demand as they were freely given. Although transport vehicles were in very short supply, she had no difficulty in arranging for several pack animals and carts to be made available for her large quantities of luggage. Bougainville had heard of her departure on the evening of September 11 and immediately wrote to de Blau, an officer under his command at Jacques-Cartier, instructing him to keep the desirable Madame de Vienne there when she arrived.[23]

No evidence exists to suggest the nature of Bougainville's relationship with Madame de Vienne, nor that they engaged in anything other than dinner. Whether he took refuge from the strain of the past month in a night of oblivion in her arms, or merely paid gentlemanly courtesies to a friend and returned to Cap Rouge, is not known. For whatever reason, Bougainville did not see, or at least did not respond to, the extraordinary industry around *Sutherland* that night.

Wolfe's troops dropped down the river to the Anse au Foulon, misleading watchful sentries who were expecting Cadet's boats by replying in French to their challenges. They made a successful landing just below the cove that nonetheless allowed nimble advance troops to scale the 175-foot bluff face, overwhelm Vergor's small detachment at the top of the Anse au Foulon, and open the way for Wolfe's main force to land and struggle its way up onto the plains above. The British battalions formed a long, thin ribbon of red in the drizzly morning light that was soon visible to the astonished French in the city. A short assault by American "provincial" troops took the Samos battery, silencing its brief storm of firing, and Wolfe had the setting for the battle he wanted.

By the full light of day, seven British battalions could be seen drawn up in battle order across the Plains of Abraham, blocking [the road west] a little less than a mile from Quebec's western wall. Behind them, five more battalions were busy improving the path, guarding the landing, and harrying Canadian and Indian skirmishers out of the woods and cornfields. At the cove a detachment of sailors manhandled a pair of brass six-pounders up the trail. More than twenty sail of ships rode at anchor in the river. Wolfe's luck, always uncommonly good, had held.[24]

Montcalm, awake all night at the Beauport defences because of a British bombardment and feigned landing on that shore, received the news with some astonishment just after he had been able to fall asleep for a few moments. Riding immediately to the city, he gave orders for his regular regiments to form line *outside* the city walls to the west, facing the British, and tried to decide what to do. At 6:45 a.m., a messenger was sent galloping off to Bougainville at Cap Rouge, Montcalm knowing full well that it would take at least three hours for Bougainville to march three thousand men in good order to Quebec. Montcalm pondered, agonized over whether to wait for Bougainville, and then decided to attack.

> We cannot avoid action; the enemy is entrenching, he already has two pieces of cannon. If we give him time to establish himself, we shall never be able to attack him with the sort of troops we have. Is it possible that Bougainville doesn't hear all that noise?[25]

Bougainville clearly had not heard the brief thunder of the Samos battery, and his journal is very limited in describing what took place, other than obliquely confirming Montcalm's estimate of the time it would take for Bougainville to fall in his column and send it trudging for Quebec:

> [The British] surprised a post half a league from Quebec. I was not informed of it until nine in the morning. I marched at once, but when I came within range of the battle, our army was beaten and

> in retreat. The entire English army advanced to
> attack me. I retreated before them and posted
> myself so as to cover the retreat of our army
> [toward Montreal].[26]

The truth of what had taken place was somewhat more complex, and certainly did not confront Bougainville with "the entire English army." It would come to be seen as either a demonstration of commendable prudence and forethought by Bougainville — or a missed opportunity that might have nullified Wolfe's precarious victory.

Wolfe's long waiting line of infantry had been enduring not only a miserable, drizzling rain but the sharpshooting of warriors and militiamen hidden in trees beyond their position, as well as the guns Montcalm had brought to bear. Wolfe ordered his men to lie down, deceiving Montcalm into thinking they were entrenching, and spurring him on to the attack. Wolfe had gambled to get his linear battle, but in so doing had placed his line where they were vulnerable to a simultaneous attack from Montcalm in the front and Bougainville in the rear. But Montcalm did not — perhaps could not — wait that long, and at about 10 a.m. he ordered forward his mixed line of French regular infantry, colony troops and militia. With a cheer they surged toward the waiting, motionless British. Bougainville, marching quickly from Cap Rouge, would still be more than an hour away.

The climax of Montcalm's advance, when it came, has been examined with great authority by many fine historians, including the Canadians Julian Gwyn and Donald Graves; no description here could do it full justice. In sum, the French line came on toward the British unevenly, stopping to fire and advancing again, the irregular loading habits of the militia mixed amidst the regular battalions throwing into disorder any precision in their movements. In two shallow, wide columns the French surged in on Wolfe, and the latter held his fire until the French were virtually within pistol range; then, three thunderstroke volleys of the British infantry halted and shattered the French line. When the British advanced through the roiling smoke to close with the bayonet, the survivors of the French line broke and ran for the gates of Quebec. A wholesale slaughter of the fleeing French regulars was prevented only by the desperate bravery of pockets of *canadiens* who, before they were overwhelmed and cut to pieces, held off the surging British as the European French streamed in through the city gates. Montcalm suffered mortal wounds and collapsed within the walls, unaware that his conqueror, Wolfe, had been killed on the battlefield at the moment of his victory.[27]

Bougainville, with some three thousand men, was now approaching from the west, his blue-coated cavalry ranging ahead. As they approached the Anse au Foulon, the cavalry reported that the Samos battery and a stone house nearby were occupied by British troops, possibly American "provincials." Bougainville now had a tactical choice to make: leave a force to deal with the Americans and go on with his main body to Quebec, or halt his advance until the Samos site was taken. Uncertain as to what he would face at Quebec, and unwilling to risk leaving an insecure position in his rear, Bougainville opted for caution and halted his column while his advance troops, at some cost of casualties and time, dispensed with the Americans. The move did serve to mitigate risk, but it added a delay — perhaps a critical one — to his arrival on the battlefield ahead. The city was still held by the French under de Ramezay, the British were in a disorganized state after their rush in pursuit of Montcalm's fleeing army, and Bougainville's column, if it had arrived sooner — even at the height of the battle itself — might have provided a different ending to the day's events. Bougainville advanced to the plains to confront the British, but found a red-coated line awaiting him. In the moments before Bougainville's arrival, Wolfe's surviving unwounded brigadier, Townsend, had realized that the army was disintegrating into an orgy of slaughtering the remaining pockets of resisting *canadiens* and looting the bodies that littered the field. He sent runners with orders to halt the pursuit of the French, reassemble the battalions and restore some semblance of order. This had begun to happen just as Bougainville's cavalry appeared at the western edge of the fields. Had Bougainville arrived even a half-hour earlier, his three thousand infantry might have inflicted a disastrous reverse on the British, and the history of the Seven Years' War in North America might have taken a very different turn.

Townsend, however, had in fact restored enough control to be able to turn and face Bougainville with at least two battalions and two field guns, and was feverishly adding more by the minute. Bougainville surveyed the thin but growing line and the uncertain scene behind it. He still outnumbered Townsend's line by two to one. His battalions were fit and capable, and had won against the British at Pointe-aux-Trembles. But he made a decision not to attack, and instead faced his column about, retiring into the shelter of the Sillery woods in his rear. The question now arises: why? It may have been a professional assessment of the need to maintain an intact "force in being," still able to keep open the supply routes to the west and able to form the nucleus around which a rebuilt French army could form; it may have been a moment when his training in North American warrior warfare, with its abhorrence of the open-field battle, had arisen in him; or it may have been a simple failure of nerve. His journal is silent. But his decision allowed Wolfe's precarious toehold to become a firm grip.

> In calling off the pursuit [of Montcalm's troops] Townsend saved the Day for the British. Even though later critics would denounce him for betraying Wolfe's boldness and success, Townsend's prudence and presence of mind enabled him to face down [Bougainville's] comparatively well-rested force [that had] the capacity to wreak havoc on his still scattered, disorganized command.[28]

It was Bougainville's decision that gave Townsend those precious moments to re-establish control. The decision may have helped cost France the colony, or at least prevented a far more favourable outcome for France in a war that was for all intents and purposes lost. Bougainville may have paid a remarkably dear price, not only for his caution at the Samos battery, but for those moments of oblivion in

Madame de Vienne's warm and naked little body.

Word reached him in his camp the next day that Montcalm had died. He would write to Madame Hérault de Séchelles:

> My heart is wounded to its tenderest depths. Monsieur le Marquis de Montcalm fought a campaign worthy of Turenne himself, and his death is our supreme misfortune.[29]

For Vaudreuil at Beauport, confusion and lack of knowledge about Bougainville's movements left him immobile and irresolute until, as evening approached, he decided to call a council of war and seek the advice of the professional military men. The council recommended a westward withdrawal by the army, skirting north around the city — before the walls of which Townsend was industriously throwing up siege entrenchments — and then a march westward to Jacques-Cartier, a distance of about twenty-five miles. This move, which Bougainville's force could cover simply by holding his position in the Sillery woods, would allow the remaining supplies at Batiscan to be protected, and when Bougainville's force also retired to Jacques-Cartier, Vaudreuil could turn command of the force to the Chevalier de Lévis, who was hurrying downriver from Montreal. Lévis could then decide what to do. Vaudreuil had no illusions about the ability of the besieged city to resist the British, however; as he began his westward march he left draft terms of surrender in the hand of the superior there, de Ramezay. Vaudreuil was right: on September 18, 1759, the city capitulated and the British army occupied it, to be faced with the problem of how to defend it in the face of certain French counterattack.[30]

At Jacques-Cartier, Lévis had arrived and made no bones about his scorn for Vaudreuil's retreat and Bougainville's lateness and hesitancy. He ordered the army back on the road, and as he came upon Bougainville's pickets he ordered Bougainville's cavalry to ride ahead with bread bags over their saddles and get supplies into the city. Lévis hoped to attack the besieging army from the rear, accurately seeing the Plains of Abraham fight as merely an engagement lost, not a war; but he was grimly dismayed to have the cavalry lather back to report that the Union Flag flew over the city, and that it had capitulated. With no siege artillery, Lévis had no choice but to withdraw again to Jacques-Cartier and consider what to do next.[31]

Before Lévis withdrew, he sent Bougainville into the captured city under a flag of truce to clarify the terms under which it had surrendered and to secure good treatment for French prisoners and wounded. Bougainville was greeted with civility and warmth by Townsend, who had allowed the honours of war to the surrendering small garrison and in many other respects acted with great restraint toward the French military and civilian population alike. Bougainville negotiated the release of senior French officers on parole to Montreal and medical care for the sick and wounded, and arranged with Townsend a means of ensuring that firewood and what meagre foodstuffs were available could be brought into the city for the population. When he left the city, Townsend wrote him warmly, "[I]n spite of the many friends you have in England, I beg of you to allow me the honour of interesting myself on your behalf and on that of your acquaintances." In a war characterized by horror and pitiless slaughter, it was a glimpse of civility and goodwill that said much about Townsend, but more about Bougainville, for whom the constructive arts seemed again more fitting than the destructive.[32]

The negotiations and the privations were, however, both lengthy, and Bougainville's fatigue had increased to the point that, at the end of October, when Vaudreuil decided to move the seat of government to Montreal, Bougainville was detached from Lévis's army at Jacques-Cartier, ordered to Montreal and told to go to bed. He wrote to Madame Hérault de Séchelles:

> The time [for this] has come. I have spent close on eighty sleepless nights, suffered indescribable fatigues and gone through miseries of a kind unknown in Europe.[33]

In the same letter, he wrote of his hope that he would be home before long, and able to see his adoptive brother, Jean-Baptiste, who had recently married. (He would not know until months later that his *chère maman* was in deep mourning for her son, who had been killed at the Battle of Minden at the beginning of August.) And he had made a difficult personal decision: whether to spare her the difficulties of being a French officer's consort as the English approached, or to please Madame Hérault, or simply because affection had waned, Bougainville had ended his relationship with his Shawnee wife, Ceuta:

> Your child has broken off the relationship which displeased you and deserves at least that you feel sorry for him.... I hope you will be happy with your child.[34]

In his writings, there is no evidence of a deeper remorse over the end of his link to Ceuta; perhaps, in the manner of many Europeans in colonial North America, it was no more to Bougainville than an arrangement of convenience that suited both parties. Whether its end was amicable or tragic — at least for Ceuta — cannot be determined. But it did leave a lasting mark in North America.

> During a trip which I made in 1811 from Pittsburgh to St. Louis on the Mississippi, at Cape Girardeau on this same river I ran into an Indian chief named Lorimer calling himself the son of M. de Bougainville, which was confirmed.... This man, born in Canada, was attracted while very young to [the Shawnees], which he joined and followed their hunting and wars. He had acquired for himself such a great reputation for skill and courage that he had become one of their primary war chiefs.[35]

The Shawnee was the tribe of the great chief Tecumseth, and although it remains to be documented, there is a strong possibility that this son of Bougainville fought alongside Tecumseth in the defence of Canada during the War of 1812, and that descendants remain, in both Canada and the United States, of the union between Louis-Antoine and Ceuta, which dissolved as New France collapsed around them.

The winter of 1759–60 was even colder than the one before, and in Montreal soldier and civilian alike endured not only the arctic conditions but also the threat of famine and want: food supplies were scarce and exorbitantly priced. Bougainville recovered his physical health, but diverted his gloom with gambling and attendance at a few brave-faced balls and salons — Madame de Vienne is not mentioned — in anticipation of the decisive season of 1760.[36]

The energetic Lévis made adjustments to the command structure as spring and its fateful campaigning approached. With Montcalm dead, Lévis was now military commander, and Bourlamaque was brought up from the small frontier post at Île-aux-Noix to be second in command. Bougainville received orders at the end of March to replace him at Île-aux-Noix. This small island, some six miles to the north of the opening of the Richelieu into the expanses of Lake Champlain, was the key remaining defence against the northward invasion route up the Champlain Valley, once Carillon (Ticonderoga) and Crown Point had been taken. Meanwhile, Lévis assembled his army and its modest remaining equipment and marched again for Quebec, even before the snows had melted. If France could get even a few ships up the river and retake the city, perhaps Canada could be held long enough to remain French in the inevitable peace negotiations. Bougainville's journal drily summarizes the results:

> The speed of [Lévis's] march surprised the enemy. Murray, Governor of Quebec, came out with his troops, was well beaten on the same terrain where we had been September 13, 1759, lost his field artillery, and was forced to re-enter the place. [The French] at once started the siege, that is to say that in order to be open to no reproaches in case aid

came from France, they started the trenches in the snow and put in position a dozen twelve-pounders (there were no others) against a place defended by a numerous garrison and more than one hundred cannon of heavy calibre. The arrival of an English squadron decided the matter.[37]

British sea power, and its victories in European and North Atlantic waters, had made impossible a successful French effort to support Lévis and Vaudreuil. Both armies at Quebec that spring of 1760 waited apprehensively to see what flag would fly over the first ships up the river after the ice vanished. When the first frigate appeared in the basin and proved to be British, Murray's jubilant garrison fired their artillery in wild salutes for over an hour. For Lévis, there was no further hope, even given his brilliant defeat of Murray outside the walls at what would come to be known as the Battle of Ste-Foy. The French withdrew toward Montreal to await the inevitable, leaving vast quantities of kit and equipment strewn about their abandoned positions.

Bougainville, meanwhile, was facing his own challenges. As he took up his command of the garrison at Île-aux-Noix, his reputation was being maligned by Vaudreuil in a series of letters the latter wrote to France, preparing a defence for the accusations that would inevitably follow Canada's defeat. Vaudreuil did not mince words:

> From the time of Montcalm's arrival in this colony, down to the time of his death, he did not cease to sacrifice everything to his boundless ambition. He sowed dissension among the troops, tolerated the most indecent talk against the government, attached himself to the most indecent people, used various means to corrupt the most virtuous and when he could not succeed, became their cruel enemy.… He, and Bougainville his aide-de-camp, defamed honest people, encouraged insubordination and closed their eyes to the rapine of his soldiers.[38]

Somewhere in all the ill-feeling and counteraccusations that were beginning to riddle the administration of New France, the whiff of an idea was surfacing that Bougainville displayed less ardour as a soldier than he might — particularly before Quebec, when he might have dissolved the advantage Wolfe had gained so precariously for the British on the Plains of Abraham. If the accusation was not concrete, it may have found fertile soil in Bougainville's own mind and heart, contributing to the determined energy he seemed to direct in future years toward justifying himself. That energy would lead to some remarkable achievements, but for the moment he grappled with the enmity of his immediate superiors, the looming threat of overwhelming attack, and the underlying knowledge that the cause of France in Canada might well be doomed. He could have been excused a certain gloom.

The 1760 campaign of the British involved a three-pronged major movement against Montreal. Murray would march westward from Quebec with as many men as he could spare from his garrison, secure in the knowledge that the Royal Navy held the river behind him and would bring additional troops from the occupation force at Louisbourg. From the south, an army of some 3,500 men under Brigadier General William Haviland would move up the Champlain Valley from Crown Point toward Montreal. And from the west, the overall commander, Jeffrey Amherst, would move from Albany to Oswego, then descend the St. Lawrence eastward to Montreal with an overwhelming force of 12,000 men that would prevent a French escape westward. The hope and intention was for these three forces to converge at Montreal and force the final capitulation of New France.[39]

The British plan worked with remarkable precision, given the uncertainty of travel and the difficulties of supply, communication and coordination that bedevilled military commanders in North America. It was not until August, however, that both Amherst's western army and Haviland's southern one reached the last serious obstacles to their respective advances on Montreal. For Amherst, it was the sturdy little French fortification of Fort Lévis, on an island in the St. Lawrence just downriver from present-day Prescott,

Ontario. And for Haviland, it was Bougainville's small fort on the low, swampy island of Île-aux-Noix in the Richelieu River. On August 16, both British commanders deployed their forces to sweep away these last obstacles.

Île-aux-Noix is not a large place, and in 1760 did not boast a large fortification. The island was about 2,000 yards by 300, the fortification a low and simple affair. But its few guns dominated the narrow river and the rough cart tracks along its banks, and Bougainville had the added benefit of work done before his arrival by French engineers, who had built dams that turned the banks of the river into swampy morasses. In addition, Bougainville positioned two armed vessels that were attached to the post, a schooner and a radeau — a kind of scow-like gun platform — "below," or on the Montreal side of the island, to prevent Haldimand from sending his own floating gun platform, the *Ligonier*, unchallenged down the river past the island. With some 1,500 men and no more than two weeks' provisions, Bougainville settled in to await Haldimand's attack.[40]

Haldimand was in position to begin a bombardment of Île-aux-Noix on August 19, and the rain of mortar shells and round shot, carried on relentlessly and at a tremendous rate of fire, soon pounded the place to a splintery rubble in which Bougainville watched his casualties mount and fired back when he could in the few moments when it was safe to peer out over the parapets. Finally, on August 25, the British sent in a boat party at night that managed, under the covering storm of shot and shell, to get aboard and "cut out" the schooner and the radeau, taking away Bougainville's remaining means of blocking Haviland's advance down the river.

Bougainville determined to get as many of his little garrison out as possible, and devised a scheme that relied as much on the humanity of the British as it did guile. On the night of August 27, Bougainville slipped out of the fort with the garrison, leaving forty wounded men whose orders were to open fire on the British the next morning as a diversion, and then surrender as and when the moment was right. In the few boats that survived,

Bougainville ferried the remainder of his garrison to the shore, then attempted to march for Montreal. His local guides, however, became confused by the swampy morasses and altered shoreline caused by the engineers' dams, and by dawn, when the wounded faithfully blasted off a few rounds for the sake of honour and then hoisted a surrender flag, an exhausted Bougainville and his troops were still floundering in the mud, barely a mile away. Narrowly escaping Haldimand's light troops, Bougainville used the daylight to finally orient himself, and he and his muddy little force squelched back to Montreal with Haldimand in leisurely pursuit behind him. It had been a creditable defence, if not a heroic one, and Bougainville had managed to save most of his garrison, for which he — and the wounded men he left behind — deserved that credit.[41]

To the west, a truly heroic stand was being made by the defenders of Fort Lévis, which was almost invisible under a cloud of smoke and debris and the flashes of shell bombs or the splintery halos that flew high as round shot from Amherst's accompanying vessels tore at the log-and-earthwork ramparts. Finally, at about the same time Bougainville slipped away from Île-aux-Noix, Amherst's horde overwhelmed the Fort Lévis garrison, and by the first week of September, the French were pent up inside the walls of Montreal. Vaudreuil and Lévis had to contemplate the chances of a successful defence with three thousand men, virtually no supplies, the desertion of the warriors to neutrality or the British cause — facing a British army of just under ten times their number, and which commanded the river. The issue was not in doubt; if Canada was to remain French, it would have to be won back at the treaty table, not by musket and bayonet.

Bougainville's command of English now brought him forward again. Still strained and weary from the marshy escape from Île-aux-Noix and the punishing days of bombardment that had preceded it, Bougainville was ordered by Vaudreuil to exit the city under a flag of truce and negotiate terms with Amherst. Bougainville was received with the customary courtesy, but Amherst was adamant: there would be no grant of the honours of war to the French garrison. With memories of Fort William Henry perhaps still large in his mind, Amherst demanded an unconditional surrender, the laying down rather than retention of arms, and a provision that the officers and men would not serve again during the war. It was a humiliating demand, and when Bougainville relayed it back to the garrison there was an explosion of anger amongst the officers. It mattered little that Amherst had agreed to virtually all of Vaudreuil's requests regarding the status and welfare of the civilian population, and even of the former warrior allies; the honour of the French officers had been insulted. Lévis broke his sword over his knee in frustration, and the French officers — including Bougainville — presented a memorial to Vaudreuil asking that they be granted the right to fight on in a grim last stand on Île Ste-Hélène, in the river off Montreal. Vaudreuil, hopefully with an eye to preserving what was left of his civilian and military resources from a useless bloodbath, refused. He granted the soldiers the right to burn their colours rather than surrender them to the English, then accepted Amherst's terms.

> Amherst's record of the event includes a bland recital of the clear lie the French used to salve their honour as regards the colours, a lie Amherst, as a soldier, might have understood: on the 9th, the ten French Battalions layed down their Arms, and delivered up two colours, which had been taken from Pepprels and Shirley's Regts. at Oswego. The Marquis de Vaudreuil, Generals, and the commanding officers of the Regts. all gave their words of honour, that the Battalions had not any colours; they had brought them six years ago with them, they were torn to Pieces, and finding them troublesome in this Country, they had destroyed them.[42]

In the smoke of the fires that consumed the French colours, both the idea and the reality, of a French empire in North America had come to an end. It would not be negotiated back into existence at the treaty table. Bougainville had been the messenger for the terms that brought this to pass. His journal is quiet now, and sombre, as if he carried with him some of the dark shadow of failure, of the inevitable loss he possibly felt that he could, at one moment, have prevented or delayed. He wrote, almost wistfully, to Lévis after the latter's victory at Ste-Foy:

> ... now that you have given back our honour, we shall all have to regard you as our father, and even should you not succeed in recapturing the town, you will still be covered in glory... there is nothing new here, we go on with our work while you are winning battles.[43]

As the autumn turned the trees along the magnificent thousand-mile stretch of the St. Lawrence shades of red, gold, amber and brown, Bougainville and the other French metropolitan officers, along with what remained of their troops, were embarked in British ships to undertake the long, dispirited voyage home across the grey Atlantic to France. Vaudreuil and the Canadian leadership would follow a year later, leaving the *habitants* to make their peace alone with the invader who was now there to stay. Before the snows began to fall across northern Europe, a gaunt, dispirited and exhausted Bougainville was entering Paris and making his way to the Hérault de Séchelles home. There, he was soon in the comforting embrace of his *chère maman*, grieving with her the loss of Jean-Baptiste, and pouring out to her for hours on end the story of what he had experienced. For the moment, war and fighting, and their dreadful costs, were over, and he had little grasp of what the future might bring as he sank into the embrace of home. It would have surprised him to learn that North America and its inhabitants would figure again in his life — and provide the means whereby the cloud of responsibility that had settled over him since that moment of hesitation before Quebec would be lifted, and dispersed with more dramatic impact than he could have imagined.

Chapter Five

A New Beginning:
Settling Acadians in the Falklands

Soon after Bougainville arrived home in December of 1760, he set about fulfilling one of the promises he had made to himself: that of securing some kind of monument to Montcalm, whose loss he still felt deeply more than a year after his death. He wrote to Montcalm's mother, the Marquise de St-Véran, and asked her to accept not only his condolences but his request for more information about Montcalm. With this in hand, he went to the *Académie des Inscriptions et Belles-Lettres* and had their scholars write a formal epitaph for Montcalm. He then wrote to Prime Minister William Pitt, asking that the epitaph be engraved on Montcalm's tomb in Quebec. In a gracious reply, Pitt agreed, and Bougainville had paid one debt to Canada.[1]

The war, however, raged on in the European theatre, and Bougainville now began a long and dispiriting process of writing to London and applying for release from his parole, without which he could not, as an honourable officer and gentleman, take up arms, a proscription he had given his word to obey. Madame Hérault de Séchelles was distraught: war had taken her natural son, and she had no wish to lose her adoptive one. Bougainville responded to her protests by pointing at Jean-Baptiste's portrait and quietly saying, "He must be avenged." The determination within him to serve again was strong, but it may have been fuelled by darker thoughts than the pain of losing his close childhood friend. His stream of letters to London continued.[2]

Before long he was called to Versailles, where Madame de Pompadour greeted him with delighted and appreciative warmth. The influence of her intimate friend and ally, the Duc de Choiseul — soon to be minister of both war and of marine — ensured that no door was closed to him. *La Pompadour* was in the process of arranging the king's ministries into a suitable disposition of power, "reserving," as Bougainville slyly put it, "to herself only the disposition of the favours of which she was the sovereign."[3]

The nature of Bougainville's relationship with Madame de Pompadour remains uncertain. What appears definite, however, is that the battle-hardened young veteran, now with an intriguing shadow of gloom or preoccupation lancing through his normal gaiety, charmed both her and an appreciative court. The possibility that Pompadour's welcome to Bougainville extended to the intimacies of her bed may have lain behind one later accusation.

> [S]omeone started an atrocious piece of malice against me among the household of the Duc de Choiseul. The pretext of it was a too-intimate relationship with a lady of importance of which they accused me.
>
> The Duchess of Gramont received me very badly, and my disgrace with her has continued.[4]

Boudoir jealousies notwithstanding, the bewigged gallants and nymphs of the aristocratic court took far more to Bougainville's warrior record — breathlessly related by *La Pompadour* — and the gallantry of the dead hero Montcalm, than the accusations and whines of the lost colony's administrators. In that, at least, Bougainville and Montcalm had secured a victory, for when, a year after Bougainville's return, Vaudreuil and his lieutenants arrived in France, they were imprisoned in the Bastille and tried for fraud, mismanagement of the colony, and a general criminality. Only Vaudreuil managed to avoid humiliating punishment; it was a victory Montcalm would have savoured.

The inner agitation that had seemed a permanent aspect of Bougainville's character ever since his return led him to beg

Versailles for some form of honourable work, even as he redoubled his pleas to London for release from his parole. Versailles was only too happy to oblige, and appointed him as aide to the Duc de Praslin, who had been nominated to attend a possible peace conference at Augsburg in 1761. When that summit failed to materialize, Bougainville found himself once more idle, a state he apparently found almost intolerable. Raging against the limitations of the honourable code that bound him, he took out his frustrations in other ways, so much so that over 1761–62 there is a degree of nihilistic abandon to the manner in which he now allowed himself to plunge into the demimonde of Paris. There was a sudden ray of hope: in 1762, Choiseul was again in peace discussions with the British, and he had raised the question of Bougainville's parole. The British replied that Bougainville could re-enter active military service, but only in Europe, and only for the month of July.

It was a symbolic crumb, given for diplomatic reasons, but it was a chance to serve. As July opened, Bougainville was sent off with private dispatches from Versailles to Germany, and a temporary post with the armies of the Maréchal d'Estrées and the Maréchal de Soubise. It was a dangerous mission, to a degree — Bougainville suffered a leg wound galloping about in a confused skirmish with a German or British picket — but his longing to take a visible and honourable part in a major battle was frustrated. He ended the summer as an aide to the Comte de Stainville, and he cantered morosely back to Paris with various reports on the state of the armies. There would be no avenging of Jean-Baptiste's death, and no gallant record of action that would ensure his promotion and career as an army officer. There also would be no absolution for the pause before Quebec on September 13, 1759 — no cleansing of the slate of that faint, but real, chalk mark against him that may have been a constant source of unsettlement within him.

But upon his glum arrival in Paris, there was uplifting news: Choiseul had secured his complete release from parole, and he was ordered to Dunkerque to take command of a two-thousand-man formation intended to form part of an expedition against Brazil, a colony of Britain's ally, Portugal. But before he could take up the post, further news arrived, to *chère maman*'s great relief: a preliminary peace treaty had been signed on November 3, 1762, at Fontainebleau, a forerunner of the overall Treaty of Paris to be signed the following February. No battlefield glory and absolution, in Brazil or anywhere, would beckon now.[5]

Bougainville salved his renewed frustration by plunging back into the social delights and dissipations of Paris to such a degree that the metropolitan police opened a file on him. That file, by August of 1763, contained reports that he had been frequenting gambling houses and brothels, and that, while posing as a marquis, he had set up an apartment on the Rue Neuve-des-Petits-Champs in which he maintained a rotating selection of nubile young mistresses, the most notable of whom was a celebrated beauty and singer at the Opéra, Sophie Arnould.

> [She] had given command performances at Versailles, where she enchanted all who heard her. She came from an upper-middle-class family, was well educated and was distinguished for her wit in a generally witty society. "… she was sought after by all men of the society of her time who were noted for their talent, birth or fortune." Bougainville could count himself in illustrious company to have been one of her lovers.[6]

At this point in his early thirties, Bougainville was, from one perspective, launched on a single-minded pursuit of pleasure that had all the hallmarks of a deliberate attempt to blot out a disturbing past. There were new responsibilities, however, beyond keeping the police baffled about his boudoir adventures: by use of inheritance and his pay he had obtained a small estate at La Brosse, between Brie and Melun, where he had placed two cumbersome German field guns that had been shipped off to him as a gift by de Stainville, and where he now had landowner's duties to fulfill. They were less often on his mind than the delicately heaving bosom of Mlle. Arnould and her sorority — or so it seemed.

If Bougainville appeared to be dissolving into yet another debauched member of a useless *noblesse*, the reality was in fact otherwise. There was yet a fire within him to achieve something — anything — that would somehow balance the books of his Canadian experience. And there was a more profound driving force: his genuine patriotism, and his contemplation of the strategic situation of France and its momentarily victorious enemy, Britain — all could be won back at some future treaty table — and what needed to be done next. His response was unique and dramatic, and it came into being through the prod of being offered the governorship, unexpectedly, of the steaming, fever-ridden colony of Cayenne on the South American coast (later French Guiana). Bougainville explained:

> They did me the honour of offering me the governorship of Cayenne, but I declined, then having [in mind] a project which I have been permitted to carry out. England, mistress of Canada by the peace treaty, of the sea by a navy incomparably stronger than all those of the powers of Europe combined, seemed to me to desire further only establishments in the South Seas.

Command of whatever lands lay in the South Seas would cement Britain's position as master of the world, with France hopelessly unable to challenge it. And control of the access to the South Seas, whether around the Horn or by Magellan's Strait, lay in occupation of the Falkland Islands in the far South Atlantic. This point had been argued by Admiral Lord George Anson of the British Admiralty, who in 1740–44 had led a circumnavigation, and whom Bougainville knew from his days in London.

> Anson had advised his country to establish itself in the Falkland Islands, which their position rendered the key to the South Seas. What else had the English to do in the interval of such a peace than to secure a supply base which put them, at the first

outbreak of war, in the position of being the
arbiters of Europe? I believed that France should
anticipate them, and I obtained leave to make, at
my own expense and that of MM. de Nerville and
d'Arboulin [Pompadour's "Bou-bou"], one my
cousin and the other my uncle, exploration of these
islands and an establishment which would assure
France its possession.[7]

The Seven Years' War had exhausted France's resources, emptied
its treasury and deprived it of colonial possessions and possibilities in
India and North America. After 1759, the French Navy had been
shattered by the preponderance of British sea power, and France's
leading role on the European continent was threatened. But the competition with Britain was not about to go away. As the perceptive
Canadian historian Barry Gough observes:

Many French politicians and patriots regarded the
new circumstances as degrading and dangerous. The
peace established in 1763 was temporary, and the
likelihood of a return to global warfare exceedingly
high…. By virtue of the fact that government was in
no position to carry out any schemes it fell to individuals to undertake enterprises by any means they
might see fit to enhance their nation's power and
prestige. The expedition of Bougainville and the
French colonization of the Falklands stems directly
from this situation.[8]

By "establishment," Bougainville had indeed meant nothing
less than the installation of a fully-functioning French colony,
hopefully a self-supporting one, that would place France in command of the gateway to the South Seas. And as colonists he had in
mind the hardy Acadian refugees from the expulsions of 1755, who
lived almost an outcast life in little communities around French
seaports, and whose suffering at the hands of the indifferent

Vaudreuil and his *canadiens* Bougainville had witnessed at close hand at Quebec. It was a grand concept, and a strategically sound one which, depending on what was found in the vast and unknown stretches of the South Pacific, might make him instrumental in restoring France's chances of glory and success. And it derived not only from the drive for self-justification that seemed now to have overtaken Bougainville, but the imagination and concept of a wider world that had come from the hours as a youth poring over maps and charts of the world with his brother.

There was, however, a sequence of events that had to be followed. The first was to obtain an audience with Louis XV, whose permission would have to grace the effort, even if the Crown had not a sou to give to it. The king was welcoming of the idea, and duly signed a warrant authorizing Bougainville to establish a colony under the Bourbon flag in the name of France. In addition, he granted Bougainville the right to lead the expedition as a brevetted naval officer (although of the non-aristocratic *bleu* category, and not the nobility's *rouge*) in the rank of *capitaine de vaisseau* — equivalent to his army rank, which he retained, as colonel. With permissions granted and ranks bestowed, but His Most Christian Majesty providing no capital for the project, Bougainville turned to his next challenge, that of finding those funds.

Bougainville's own resources were considerable, due to his reasonably wise use of family funds, the support of patrons and the husbanding of his army pay and rents from the little estate. But to mount an expedition of settlement halfway around the world was an expenditure on a different order. The powerful government minister Choiseul was supportive of what Bougainville had in mind for a myriad of reasons, ranging from an equal patriotism to a binding personal alliance with *La Pompadour*, and he placed the material resources of the naval ministry, a huge asset, at Bougainville's service. To secure the necessary actual cash, Bougainville went to his uncle, the administrator-general of posts, Jean-Potentin d'Arboulin, and to Bougainville's cousin, M. de Nerville, who was also well off financially. With "Bou-bou" and his cousin he was successful, and the plan took shape.

> The final agreement [writes Kimbrough] was that
> Bougainville and [d'Arboulin] were to shoulder the
> principal expenses, but the king would give them
> the equipment for arming the ships and the colony,
> rigging and artillery, supplies which [the navy]
> already had and which would entail no further
> expense. Moreover, the naval and military person-
> nel to be sent were already in the king's pay, and
> the displaced Acadian families who were to form
> the nucleus of the colony had been receiving royal
> subsidies for some time.[9]

With this agreement in hand, Bougainville moved to the next
stages. At the historic port of St-Malo, he brought into being the
Compagnie de St-Malo, then contracted a regular navy officer, Nicolas
Duclos-Guyot, to supervise the construction of two ships for the company, the 300-ton small frigate *Aigle* and the 120-ton corvette *Sphinx*.
Both were ship-rigged vessels of warship design — meaning that they
carried squaresails on all three masts — the former carrying anywhere
from twelve to twenty guns and the latter eight to twelve. The command of *Aigle* would go to Duclos-Guyot for the voyage, and of
Sphinx to François Chenard de la Giraudais, a former officer in the
merchant service with a reputation for toughness. Embarked in the
two ships was to be a mountain of equipment and supplies, and
squeezed in amongst that some 130 individuals, the ship's companies
added to by a half-company of marines and three families who would
form the first core of the settlement. As the marines were Acadian in
origin, and the families both Acadian and Canadian, the enterprise for
the Falklands would have a distinctly North American tone.[10]

Through the summer of 1763, work on both ships drew to completion as Bougainville supervised the assembly of the equipment
and supplies. By August the loading of the ships could begin, and by
early September preparations were complete. Bougainville had carefully chosen his participants, not forgetting to embark scientists and
a naturalist — a Benedictine monk named Dom Pernetty, who was
to perform the dual role of chaplain and scientist.

On September 15, 1763, *Aigle* and *Sphinx* let fall their canvas and worked clear of the St-Malo harbour, steering southwestward. The voyage track was intended to take them to the Falklands by way of intended anchorages on the coast of Brazil and at Montevideo in Uruguay. To take advantage of the trade winds, the flotilla would beat its way across the Bay of Biscay and then steer to clear the Portuguese coast, angling southwestward until, off the coast of Africa, they would pick up the west-blowing Northeast Trades, follow them to the uncertain winds of the Doldrums, and then hopefully find the Southeast Trades below the equator for the run to the Brazilian coast. In Bougainville's cabin now lay the parchment, with its great wax seal and the signature of Louis XV granting him a brevet commission as *capitaine de vaisseau,* and he strode the quarterdeck of the hurrying *Aigle* in the uniform of a naval officer. He would never resume his army role, and it is not difficult to imagine his thoughts as the ships beat their way into the Atlantic, carrying him toward what he hoped would be a new beginning for France — and a vindication for himself in a new world of endeavour.[11]

The remote island group in the far South Atlantic toward which Bougainville was steering his little flotilla already had somewhat of a history in Western navigational knowledge. The group lies some three hundred miles from the South American continent, eastward off the southern parts of present-day Argentina. There are two principal islands, now known as West Falkland and East Falkland, and some two hundred islands or islets in total. The group is divided into two divisions by a strait, about twenty miles wide, that runs between them from southwest to northeast. The land is rugged, windswept and rocky, with grassy and boggy slopes rising to a mountainous interior, but without trees. In their austere, blustery ruggedness they resemble the Faeroes, the Orkneys and the Shetland Islands to the north of Britain. Of this resemblance, Bougainville had very little advance knowledge.

The credit for the discovery of the islands lies, as far as can be determined, with the Elizabethan seaman John Davis of Devon, who arrived unexpectedly on August 14, 1592. Davis was taking part in a quasi-piratical expedition into the South

Seas mounted by Thomas Cavendish, and he spent little time on the islands, pausing only to repair storm damage. He was followed in February 1594 by Sir Richard Hawkins, who tarried long enough to give the islands the name of Hawkins Maiden Land, in salute both to Queen Elizabeth and himself. Not to be outdone, the Dutch navigator Sebald de Weert sighted the islands in 1600 and named them the Sebaldines; it was, however, Hawkins' name, shortened to "Hawkinsland," that became their common name. For the rest of the seventeenth century they were largely ignored, as seamen concentrated on the Cape Horn, Magellan and Cape of Good Hope sea routes. Finally, in 1690, John Strong of England put in to the islands while operating under a "letter of marque" — permission both to conduct trade and make war, whichever proved more profitable at the moment — from the English court.

Strong knew his politics, and he named the group the Falkland Islands after the navy's treasurer, Viscount Falkland. That small ceremony complete, Strong sailed off in search of booty and business, and the islands were left alone to the gulls and penguins for another half-century.

In the first half of the eighteenth century, while Britain and France grappled with one another in the Northern Hemisphere, a contest of almost equal intensity was going on in the south, in the waters of Spain's vast dominions in Central and South America. At stake was the right to trade with these colonies, and in particular to obtain the rights to the most lucrative aspects of this trade — notably the *asiento*, the trade in slaves from West Africa. It was the aim of the British, French and Dutch seamen who fought an unending and undeclared war with one another to secure this trade, while the Spanish endeavoured to prevent that happening at the expense of their own mercantile marine. The contest was enriched by the occasional formal declaration of war with the harassed Spanish and a far more regular piracy that plundered the wealthy, ill-defended colonies of Spanish America when trade was not an option. It was during one of these periods of war (1739–48) that Britain sent a flotilla of ships around the Horn to attack Spanish colonies on the Pacific coast of

America and strike a blow at Spain's flow of wealth by attempting to intercept the fabled Manila galleon, a treasure ship that crossed the North Pacific each year from Manila to Central America, there to add its wealth to that being convoyed to Spain from America.

The flotilla was under the command of Commodore George Anson, and over the years 1740–44 he carried out his orders with remarkable material success, his flagship *Centurion* staggering home laden to the scuppers with a spectacular haul of treasure — they found, and took, the galleon — but leaving the bodies of two-thirds of his seamen in its wake, almost all victims of scurvy, the dreaded disease caused by a Vitamin C deficiency, which made extensive ocean voyaging such a lethal proposition. Four years after Anson's return, he urged in the official report of the voyage that the Falkland Islands be surveyed as a first move toward securing for Britain a port near the entrance to Cape Horn, to enable voyaging into the Pacific to be undertaken with greater ease and a less horrific cost in crews. Gough relates what occurred:

> Immediately, the Admiralty laid plans for an expedition of reconnaissance. British claims that this was a scientific pursuit did not fool the Spanish, who protested at the obvious nature of [this] foreign encroachment. The Spanish minister Carvajal made abundantly clear to the British ambassador [to Spain] Keene that "he hoped we would consider what air it would have in the world to see us planted directly against the mouth of the Straits of Magellan, ready upon all occasions to enter into the South Seas." Sensing the diplomatic consequences of the situation, and the degree of Spanish anxieties, the British government cancelled the proposed expedition.[12]

The British interest in the Falklands subsided until the close of the Seven Years' War, when the Earl of Egmont echoed Anson's arguments and championed within the Admiralty a renewed concept of placing Britain at the threshold of the South Pacific. This time, the government acted: in June of 1764, two vessels — the frigate *Dolphin* and the sloop-of-war *Tamar* — were dispatched under the command of Commodore John "Foul Weather Jack" Byron, sailing for the China Seas by way of Cape Horn. Byron's secret orders were to sail to the Falklands and stake a formal claim to them for Britain, then pass around the Horn and seek along the coastline north of California the rumoured Northwest Passage back to the North Atlantic. Byron arrived in the Falklands on January 12, 1765, anchored in a secure harbour that was duly named Port Egmont, hoisted a flag, fired guns and served out spirits to his crews to "drink the king's health" and commemorate the formal claim process. Before sailing on, he coasted a portion of the island group, named some features, then steered away. He was unaware that, up one of the sheltered sounds he did not penetrate, he would have found the healthy French post of Fort St-Louis, which Bougainville had established. Bougainville's mind had come to the same conclusion as Egmont's; but Bougainville had got there first.[13]

There had been other motivations behind Bougainville's initiative into the South Atlantic beyond simple patriotism or any desire to prove himself after the disappointments — or worse — of Canada and Germany. Even as he had indulged himself in the pleasures of dissipation in Paris to a notorious degree, his mind remained active and involved in the excitement and curiosity that were characteristic of eighteenth-century intellectual thought, with its focus on rational exploration of the world about one and the awareness, as the clouds of war slowly lifted, of the great remaining enigma of the planet's geography: the vast Southern Ocean and the concept of a balancing *Terra Australis* comparable to Northern Hemisphere land masses. Bougainville had certainly been leading a diverse life that would have him surface from the athletically sensual satisfactions of a mistress's embrace to plunge into the intellectual discussions in the most brilliant of the Parisian salons that examined and dissected the new science, notably that kept by M. and Mme. Helvétius. In a heady atmosphere of vigorous empiricism and boundless curiosity, his intellectual energy clearly keeping pace with his libido, Bougainville found himself conversing with some of the finest minds in Europe; and again and again, the question of what lay in the uncharted seas west of South America came to the fore.

> If an immense *terra australis* did in fact exist, the wealth, power and prestige accruing to the country responsible for its discovery would be incalculable.... This new land might contain heretofore unknown species of plant and animal life, the classification and description of which would serve to build a researcher's reputation in the community. The potential treasures in this lost continent never ceased to stir the minds of the adventuresome, be they politicians or scientists.[14]

As *Aigle* and *Sphinx* thrust their bows into the heavy swells of the Bay of Biscay and forged their way south, Bougainville was thus arguably being driven by three motives rather than one: the hope of gaining for France a geopolitical and colonial advantage that would make up for the losses of Canada and India; the intellectual curiosity of the scientist, mathematician and now explorer; and a deep personal desire to erase the disappointments of Canada — and a possible personal sense of failure — with a new success that would bring honour to his career. The driving energy which characterized Bougainville had as much of self-justification in its fuel as it did simple patriotism and the curiosity of the intellectual. It was a powerful mix of propellants, and it was now pushing him outward on the second great overseas enterprise of his life.

The departure of the two ships had not been without incident. One of the three initial settlement families, after boarding, had balked at the preparatory work that was expected of them. Bougainville allowed them to keep the money and goods he had advanced them — all the settlers were provided for in this way — but put them ashore near St-Malo before striking out for the South Atlantic. Bougainville's exasperated parting comment to them was succinct: "Since poverty suits you, go and live in poverty."[15]

The passage south toward Brazil was uneventful — Bougainville took full part in the bawdy and humiliating ritual of crossing the equator with good humour, which much increased his standing with the crewmen and passengers alike — and finally, on January 14, 1764, the ships dropped anchor off the island of Santa Catarina, off the coast of Brazil. The Portuguese governor was warmly welcoming, and he lavishly entertained Bougainville and his people ashore. Bougainville was to reciprocate this generosity with a dinner given under an awning rigged above *Aigle*'s quarterdeck, to the sound of "hautboys, violins and timpani." This colourful extravagance set the tone of the ships' two-week stay, during which time the work of resupplying the ships was leavened, for both the officers and the common folk, by the attractions of Brazilian hospitality. The naturalist, Dom Permetty, was enchanted by the lush, bird-and-flower-filled forests of the island, although the fear of poisonous snakes and venomous insects found those of less scientific bent satisfied to limit themselves to the *cantinas* and gardens of the settlement. When the ships finally sailed for Montevideo on December 26, they were laden with foodstuffs, fruit, livestock and other more exotic supplies — including live specimens of birds and animals, amongst them a jaguar. This last unfortunate creature did not survive the passage to Montevideo, as its roaring kept all on board constantly awake and it ate its way through a vast quantity of the precious stores.

The arrival in Montevideo was anything but welcoming; one senses Spanish unease over the purposes of the French expedition, the Bourbon bond notwithstanding. Almost as soon as the vessels had rounded up to anchor, Bougainville received a message from the governor that the expedition could expect no assistance from him. Stung, Bougainville dashed off a stiff note, very similar in wording and tone to one that James Cook of the Royal Navy would send ashore to an equally hostile viceroy at Rio de Janeiro a few years later:

Monsieur,

It is indeed hard that Frenchmen should meet from their friends the Spanish with difficulties which

they did not encounter from the Portuguese, with
whom, not so short a time ago, they were at war. I
shall put to sea at once, but I shall give an account
of this to the King my master.[16]

Bougainville had another concern as well: the small consort,
Sphinx, did not arrive for their planned rendezvous at the mouth of
the Río de la Plata. After waiting some time at the exposed anchorage, Bougainville ordered *Aigle* to move on to Montevideo, where
they would await *Sphinx*.

The stiff note to the governor broke the initial resistance of that
worthy individual to their arrival, but Bougainville continued to contend with Spanish misgivings that the French were there to trade in
contraband; only another cool note pointing out that *Aigle* and
Sphinx were king's ships, and not merchantmen or privateers, eased
that concern. Bougainville also had difficulty getting the Spanish to
agree to barter needed stores (such as construction timber) in return
for French spirits and wines — Bougainville, it seemed, had no
money the Spanish would accept, but did boast a well-stocked wine
cellar — and it took a meeting of the colony's royal council to approve
the trade in kind. The exasperated French also had to contend with
the venomous hostility of the colony's Jesuits, whose French colleagues were in the process of being expelled from France. For the
expedition's scientists, including Permetty, the Uruguayan society and
landscape offered diversions that compensated for the political difficulties. If the society was one whose most notable quality appeared to
be idleness, it also seemed to be one that enjoyed itself:

> When not enjoying a siesta, the men sat enjoying a
> cigar and listening to their womenfolk strumming the
> guitar. Dom Permetty watched closely a dance known
> as the *calenda*, introduced by slaves from the Guinea
> Coast, and with righteous Benedictine indignation
> condemns it in his journal as of a "voluptuous and
> lascivious character."[17]

Sphinx at last wandered into port at the end of December 1763, having run hard aground off the coast of Brazil and been rescued from its predicament largely through the help of Indians and black slaves. The stores were got aboard, farewells — warm and otherwise — were made to the still-apprehensive Spanish, and on January 17, 1764, the two ships steered for the Falklands. The voyage took two weeks, and on their arrival off the rugged and forbidding islands Bougainville had his little flotilla circumnavigate the group, "studying the largest island's configuration, soil properties, vegetation, fauna, fresh water resources and characteristics of its bays and inlets." After several weeks of such careful surveying, Bougainville selected a settlement site about three miles up a narrow inlet, now called Berkeley Sound, on the northeastern face of East Falkland. The settlement was to be known as Fort St-Louis.[18]

Bougainville was not entirely dismayed at the aspect of the land, but it was clear that the Falklands were not a paradise. They were, he wrote:

> ... a landscape bounded on the horizon by bleak mountains, the foreground eroded by the sea, which seems to be ever struggling for supremacy; a country lifeless for want of inhabitants; neither pasturelands nor forests for the encouragement of those who are destined to become the first colonists; a vast silence, broken only by the occasional cry of a sea monster; everywhere a weird and melancholy uniformity.[19]

The sturdy Acadian families and the troops set to with a will, however. The site soon revealed itself to be rich in peat, which could be used for fuel, and freshwater streams were everywhere. Wildfowl and fish were abundant and easily caught, and gradually, after the first hesitations, enthusiasm built amongst the little company.

Bougainville settled on a building plan very similar in concept to the Port Royal Habitation built by Samuel de Champlain and the Sieur de Monts in 1605 on Nova Scotia's Annapolis Basin, in what would become the heartland of Acadia. It would be a rectangular fortification, containing within it a kind of longhouse divided by partitions into living quarters and storage sheds. Earthworks were constructed around this structure and its courtyard, embrasures cut in the walls for the fort's fourteen guns, and an obelisk raised in the centre of the courtyard carrying the arms of France. The work was completed by April 5, 1764, and Bougainville then read to the assembled company the royal patent that appointed de Nerville as governor of the colony. A twenty-one-gun salute followed, and France was established in the South Atlantic.[20]

Three days later, on April 8, 1764, satisfied that the colony was on a sound footing, Bougainville sailed for France with his two vessels. He had also left behind a coin buried at the base of the obelisk, bearing the inscription "*Conumar tenues grandia*," — "Small though we are, we attempt a mighty task." It was a fitting motto to the imagination and effort of Bougainville's concept.[21]

The voyage home to France passed without incident; Bougainville had himself put ashore at Morlaix on June 25, where he could get to Versailles quickly while *Aigle* worked round to St-Malo, where it arrived the next day. When Bougainville arrived at the court, he was thunderstruck to learn that his champion, patron and confidante, Madame de Pompadour, had died at the age of forty-two just as Fort St-Louis was being completed in the Falklands. Deprived of her support, Bougainville was unsure what reception he would receive from the king and his ministers. Nonetheless, he obtained audiences with both Louis XV and Choiseul, yet minister of marine, and made a bold series of proposals. He reported that Fort St-Louis was established and thriving, and needed more colonists, as well as royal acceptance as a colony of France. To Bougainville's delight, the king accepted the colony as a formal French possession, agreed to a resupply mission that would transport additional settlers at the Crown's expense, and confirmed the *Compagnie de St-Malo* in its charter. It was at this point that the name *Malouines* for the islands, after St-Malo (later to be rendered in Spanish as the *Malvinas*), came into currency.

Bougainville's most contentious proposal was the negotiation with Spain of a naval agreement that would turn the South Atlantic into a "latin lake" if Britain attempted inroads there — contentious because of Spanish suspicions regarding France's intentions. As word of what Bougainville was up to filtered back to Spain from Montevideo — he had been frank with the governor as to his purpose — the Spanish ambassador to France, de Fuentes, quietly drew Choiseul aside and told him that the Franco-Spanish military alliance applied only to Europe, and that Spain would not accept the placement of a French colony anywhere within its sphere of influence. Securing a formal response to Bougainville's colony would take time, in part because the Spanish government was not entirely sure where the Falklands/Malouines actually were.

Bougainville resolved to press on and allow political considerations — and Spanish geographical bemusement — to work themselves out. In preparation for the formal validation of the St-Malo Company, Bougainville had detached *Sphinx* during the return journey from Fort St-Louis to Guadeloupe, with orders to round up a valuable cargo. *Sphinx* loyally rolled into St-Malo in early August, suitably laden with Caribbean treasures, and the company was able to turn the proceeds from the sale of the cargo toward refitting *Aigle*, securing new supplies for the colony, and recruiting fifty or more new colonists, again from among refugee Acadians. On October 6, 1764, *Aigle* steered once more for the South Atlantic. As he paced its spray-wet quarterdeck, Bougainville could have been excused a moment of inner satisfaction at his success so far.[22]

The voyage to the Malouines was again uneventful, a credit both to fair weather and the not-inconsiderable seamanship of the French, and *Aigle* rounded up to its anchor off Fort St-Louis on January 5, 1765, to gun salutes and an ecstatic welcome. To Bougainville's great joy, he found the colony healthy and thriving; vegetable gardens were flourishing, livestock were healthy, and so were the colonists, with only one death, an accident, having occurred. De Nerville, ruddy and relaxed, greeted his cousin with warmth and enthusiasm; he was clearly at home in the bracing, if rigorous, life of the colony. Soon after arriving, it was pointed out to Bougainville that the colony's small supply of building timber was exhausted: de Nerville had built new storehouses and a powder magazine and added to the fortifications. He asked if Bougainville would undertake a woodcutting voyage to the South American coast, three hundred miles distant, and Bougainville agreed. It would offer a chance to explore the approaches to both the Strait of Magellan and Cape Horn — the grim gateways to the South Pacific — and, as a side interest, there were always the rumoured giants of Patagonia to be sought out.

Aigle tacked away into the westerlies toward the Strait of Magellan; soon after entering it, they were astonished to see, riding at anchor in the mountainous, fjordlike channels, three ships flying the British ensign. *Aigle* cautiously anchored some distance away, so the nature of the British ships — whether naval or civilian — was unclear until one of them lost its moorings and was seen foundering on the rocky shoreline. Bougainville lowered *Aigle*'s boats and sent them over to assist. Thanks were tendered to him by the British Commodore, Captain John Byron — they were naval vessels, after all. Byron was himself just in from his visit to the site at Port Egmont on West Falkland, and was on his way to a two-year circumnavigation remarkable only for the fact that he survived it. Byron and Bougainville exchanged civilities, mutually refused to accept the validity of the other's claim to the Falklands/Malouines, and parted with gentlemanly courtesies, gun salutes and loosed topsails. Byron continued westward, and Bougainville made his own way more selectively into the Strait's serpentine windings until he came upon a heavily wooded cove — now Bougainville Bay — where he anchored. Bougainville and the other officers put on seamen's work clothing and joined in the physical labour of woodcutting, and for three weeks the ship's company toiled industriously to cram every foot of timber into *Aigle* that could be cut. Logs were cut and timbers hewn and floated out to *Aigle* in huge rafts, to be swayed aboard with boat tackles fastened to yardarms and stays, while, Bougainville relates:

> we also carefully lifted and carried on board more than 10,000 seedlings from trees of different ages, and the establishment of plantations on our islands was a most interesting experiment.[23]

The Patagonian natives showed up on the shoreline; they were affable and hardy souls of average height in roughly cut furs, who traded peacefully for cloth and metal and would not touch the Frenchmen's brandy. Finally, the loading was complete, and, in a consummate display of seamanship, the heavily overladen *Aigle* wallowed out of the Strait into the boisterous South Atlantic and made the three hundred mile passage safely back to Fort St-Louis, anchoring there on a blustery March 29, 1765.

As the last splintery timber was dragged off *Aigle*'s decks, Bougainville told a beaming de Nerville that there was now a practical "seaway as necessary for the support of the colony." A month later, riding considerably higher in the water, *Aigle* sailed for France, clearing the Malouine coast on April 27.

On arrival back in France, Bougainville's positive report to the king on the progress of the colony led Louis XV to approve a third supply voyage. This time, under the command of Duclos-Guyot, and consisting of *Aigle* and another supply ship, the *Étoile*, the company's flotilla made a successful reprovisioning voyage to Fort St-Louis, including another timber-cutting expedition to the Strait of Magellan. With the successful return of the ships to France, the prosperity and future of the South Atlantic colony — and the *Compagnie de St-Malo* — seemed assured.

Bougainville, however, was about to receive a rude shock. Choiseul called him in, and the news he imparted was not good.

> Choiseul told him bluntly the colony would have to be turned over to the Spanish. He set forth to Bougainville Madrid's claims, which he, the marine minister, accepted; she had not had time to colonize those islands herself because her commitments on the South American mainland were so great and pressing; if she permitted the French colony to remain, then she could not object if the British colonized other uninhabited islands off the coast.[24]

Bougainville was stunned, but he was not about to give up his endeavour, and what he thought it meant for France, without a fight. He wrote a passionate and reasoned document to Choiseul, arguing why the colony should be retained: the islands were the stepping stone to the Pacific world, a strategic base for French operations in the South Atlantic in support of a Spanish ally, a potential home for a superb fishery, and they had been empty — although the British, with their as yet unpopulated Port Egmont site, would debate that point. Choiseul listened, then directed Bougainville to discuss things with the Spanish, who invited him to Madrid.

With some resignation, Bougainville rode to Madrid on horseback — in that year, 1766, he would make the round trip twice — to find that, as Choiseul likely knew, his case was already lost. The Spanish were adamant that the colony was to become theirs, and Choiseul had agreed. It was Bougainville's task, his orders now read, to negotiate the terms. He found the Spanish generous, and financial ruin did not, as he had feared on his long canter across the Pyrenees, stare him in the face. The Spanish began by stating that they were not obliged to compensate Bougainville, but then they did so. Moreover, they agreed to reimburse the costs of the settlers' support; the equipment and materials, including the buildings, to be left behind; the cost of relocating those settlers not wishing to remain under Spanish rule; and the personal expenses and investments of Bougainville, de Nerville and d'Arboulin, with 5 percent interest added. They were generous terms indeed, and Bougainville agreed. The Spanish were to take possession of the islands as of January 1, 1767.

Bougainville returned to Paris with the Spanish terms, which pleased the king and Choiseul; a major diplomatic row with a vital, if lethargic, ally had been avoided. To compensate Bougainville, he was offered the governorship of the Indian Ocean islands of Mauritius and Réunion, recently taken over by the Crown from the India Company. The Spanish, however, interjected that they would accept only Bougainville as France's agent for the actual transfer of the colony in the South Atlantic. Choiseul and the king agreed, as they now had another task to offer Bougainville, if he would accept it. He did so with alacrity.

France had awakened to Bougainville's message about the importance of projecting itself into the Pacific, even if the Malouines — now the Malvinas — had had to be sacrificed on the altar of the Spanish alliance. The British had become more active in the South Pacific, with several circumnavigations under way, and at least one British warship had appeared off Fort St-Louis, threatening a defiant de Nerville with eviction from British territory. To carry out the Malouines transfer, France would indeed send Bougainville. But the king and Choiseul had other plans: the royal treasury had paid for the construction of a fine new frigate at St-Malo, the twenty-six-gun *La Boudeuse.* The intent was to send it, with a storeship, to carry out the transfer of authority to the Spanish at Fort St-Louis and supervise the evacuation in Spanish ships of those colonists who wished to leave. But then, *La Boudeuse* and the accompanying storeship would be sent into the South Pacific on a voyage of exploration, discovery, scientific investigation and the examination of what opportunities might lie for France in that vast, largely uncharted ocean. The voyage was then to be completed with a circumnavigation and return to France. The court asked if Bougainville would accept command of the expedition.

The court would soon have its answer. In a matter of months, Bougainville would be outbound into a largely unknown ocean and, as the first French commander to be offered such a stunning challenge, a circumnavigation. A glittering ocean, rich with unknown possibilities, lay before him, as did the prospect of yet achieving the distinction he had pursued, but which in his own mind, at least, had eluded him. He was soon on his way to St-Malo to begin the preparations.

Chapter Six
The Great World Voyage

Although Louis-Antoine de Bougainville had pried the lid off of French interest in the potential of the South Pacific, he was opening a sea chest into which the French had already peered, to a degree. In 1663 the cleric Jean Paulmier de Courtonne published a work in which he identified himself as the descendant of a native from the tropics named Essomericq, who had been brought back to France in 1505 by a French navigator, de Gonneville, after an attempted voyage to the East Indies. De Gonneville's description of the land where Essomericq had been found did not match any descriptions of places encountered by the Dutch in their eastward explorations. De Courtonne therefore insisted that his ancestor could only have come from a balancing *Terra Australis* that offset the weight of the northern continents. His book became a subject for intellectual discussion to the extent that geographers claimed that the "Great South Land," as it came to be known, would have to lie at approximately 45 degrees south latitude in either the South Atlantic or the South Pacific, and should therefore have a climate as temperate as that of France, which lay at a similar northern latitiude.[1]

The concept was picked up by such intellectuals as Pierre-Louis Moreau de Maupertuis and Charles de Brosses, who argued both for the necessary existence of the Great South Land and its potential for France. It had been de Brosses's *Histoire des navigations aux terres australes* that had planted in the youthful Bougainville the first imaginings of a vast, temperate southern continent that awaited claim and settlement. The French East India Company went so far as to send off two ships in 1738, under Jean-Baptiste Charles Bouvet de Lozier, to explore the South Atlantic in the vicinity of 40 degrees south and claim anything he found. His two ships, *Aigle* and *Marie* (the former was not the same vessel as Bougainville's first expedition ship), searched about in wintry conditions in the South Atlantic and glimpsed a grim, rockbound shore which Bouvet named Cape Circumcision, and which he took to be a jutting promontory of de Gonneville's *Terra Australis*. The discovery was enough for a number of geographers, including Guillaume de l'Isle, to add it as part of a disconnected shoreline on a 1740 chart. Philippe Buache produced an atlas in 1755 that went further, showing it as the tip of a large continent in the South Atlantic between Africa and South America.[2]

Bougainville's own voyages into the South Atlantic had revealed no sizeable land mass. Nonetheless, in arguing the same case Anson had made, and pleading for France to get ahead of British expansion into the Pacific, Bougainville was still drawing on an established concept in French geographical and intellectual thought. His contribution to the process was to convince the king and his ministers that now was the moment to pursue that geographical ephemera in France's best interests — before it would be forever too late.

It was at this time, as Bougainville made his preparations for the voyage, that the wisdom of applying for naval rank became clear. There had been some simple practicalities to begin with: with colonial affairs coming under the ministry of the marine, possession of a naval rank had made it easier to develop the Falkland colony, and he had already been thinking about a possible world voyage — which, reason demanded, called for a naval identity. It had become evident to him as well that changes in the nature of the French army were likely to leave him with few promotional prospects. The losses of the Seven Years' War had increased tensions between aristocratic and middle-class officers, each blaming the other for the defeats. However, the Maréchal de

Belle-Isle, the incoming minister of war, enacted reforms that limited senior rank to the promising members of the nobility and largely excluded the middle class. To transfer to the navy was to move to a service where, to a degree, merit should permit upward progress through the command ranks. It was also evident that in any future war with Britain — an inevitability — a resurgent navy would be necessary to France's survival.

Bougainville's friend and mentor, Choiseul, was still minister of marine, and he instituted naval reforms that were counter to Belle-Isle's: the aristocratic *rouge* naval officers (so called for their unique, all-scarlet uniforms) who had performed poorly were weeded out, and non-noble officers of the *bleu* (again, for their predominant uniform colour), like Bougainville, were encouraged to join and advance in the navy. This focus on merit was to transform the French navy, as events during the American Revolution would show, but it also increased the bitterness the remaining *rouge* officers harboured toward Bougainville and his middle-class peers — they were sneered at as *les intrus*, the intruders. Until the French Revolution swept it away, Bougainville would continue to suffer from such bigotry, an enmity held at bay only by his abilities and achievements and the benevolence of ministers who knew a competent man when they saw one.[3]

The prospects for a successful world voyage were improved when he learned that the smaller vessel of the two given him would not have to remain at the Malouines, transporting colonists to the mainland or back to France, but would be available as a storeship for the entire circumnavigation. The Spanish had offered to transport the departing colonists in their own vessels. This was a vital change, and Bougainville knew it.[4]

He arrived in Nantes on November 1, 1766, then moved to inspect his frigate, *La Boudeuse*, a short distance up the Loire at Mindin. His storeship, the corvette-sized *Étoile*, was in refit at Rochefort, and a sailing plan had been suggested that provided for the two ships' rendezvous in South America, at either the Falklands or on the mainland coast, since *Étoile* would not be ready to sail in company with *La Boudeuse*. The final preparations, and the storing and loading of the frigate with the immense amounts of supplies necessary for such an ambitious expedition, were eventually completed, and Bougainville would sail on November 15, 1766, bound for the South Atlantic.[5]

La Boudeuse had been begun in June of 1765 at the Indret shipyard, not far from Nantes, and had been launched in March 1766. It was a warship in design, a twenty-six-gun frigate of 960 tons, square-rigged on all three masts. Its total complement, when all in Bougainville's scientific entourage had been accommodated, would come to some 220 souls. Although sleek in design and impressive in appearance — French warships were generally better and faster sailers than their English and Dutch counterparts — *La Boudeuse* was nonetheless a warship rather than a sturdy, all-purpose expedition ship, and its "sea trials" would have to take place during the voyage, not before. Although commanding a frigate would give Bougainville prestige in Spanish eyes during the handover of the Malouines, his mind was on the rigours of the immense voyage they were undertaking, and in the initial stages of the trip the frigate proved so difficult to handle that Bougainville gave serious thought to continuing in his smaller but proven storeship *Étoile* and sending the frigate home after the colony transfer. Only after *La Boudeuse* overcame its technical problems to an acceptable degree would he relent and take it round the world.[6]

The other vessel of the expedition was the ship-rigged storeship, *Étoile*, considerably smaller at 480 tons than *La Boudeuse* but a proven veteran of the South Atlantic. Originally a merchant vessel bought for the navy in 1762, *Étoile* had performed reliably, if not spectacularly, on voyages to Cayenne in 1764 and to the Malouines themselves, first in 1765. Carrying 120 men, it would prove to be a reliable and manoeuvrable consort for *La Boudeuse* on the voyage. It was hoped that *Étoile*'s refit before the voyage would ensure that the circumnavigation would not suffer from unreliable and ill-prepared ships. Both vessels would survive the expedition and serve the French navy honourably for some time thereafter, with *Étoile* being paid off from naval service in 1778 and *La Boudeuse* serving through to the Revolutionary era in 1800.[7]

If the two ships selected for the circumnavigation were the best that French resources allowed for at the time, the officers who were selected to sail with Bougainville, and whom he had a major role in selecting, were of no less quality. There was, to begin with, no need to appoint a "flag captain," under Bougainville, to command *La Boudeuse* — Bougainville was already a competent navigator by virtue of his command of mathematics and knowledge of cartography, and he had proven an astonishingly apt student of seamanship and ship handling. Seasoned by the repeated voyages to the South Atlantic, his seamanship had begun with the return voyage to Canada on *La Chézine* in the spring of 1759. On that voyage he had befriended one of the ship's officers, Nicolas-Pierre Duclos-Guyot, and had virtually become his pupil in an intensive introduction into square-rig seamanship and the responsibilities of command at sea. Bougainville did not come to this knowledge "through the hawse hole," as the expression went — rising from the rank of seaman to officer by experience and merit — but it seems he was a natural sailor with an instinctive competence. Diligent application during the long South Atlantic voyages combined with his navigational ability, so that by 1766 he lacked nothing in the formal preparation of a naval captain except the key factor of experience. Nonetheless, Bougainville took *La Boudeuse* to sea having fully qualified — on paper, at least — to serve as its captain, a remarkable professional achievement that the minister of marine was only too happy to confirm.

Bougainville knew, however, that he needed men to support him who had the experience he lacked. He turned therefore to the appointment of the loyal friend Duclos-Guyot as first lieutenant (or *seconde*, in French parlance) in the frigate, with the rank of *capitaine de brûlot*, or fireship commander. As he hoped, Bougainville would find him a pillar of reliability, describing him as:

> ... assuredly one of the best [seamen] in Europe, and few could claim such extensive periods of service both in peace and in wartime. His success

in everything he has undertaken makes him worthy
of recommendation.[8]

There were five young aristocrats in *La Boudeuse's* wardroom,
serving under Bougainville and Duclos-Guyot, both of whom were
bleu officers. All former members of the elite *gardes de la marine*,
the aristocratic preparatory body for aspiring naval officers, they
were Lamothe-Barace de Bournand, *enseigne*; De Fulques
d'Oraison, also an *enseigne*; Gratet de Bouchage, *enseigne*, who
would die during the voyage; Jean-Baptiste-François de Suzannet;
and Cramezel de Kerhue, the last two coming aboard as cadets, but
who were promoted to *enseigne* during the voyage. The officers'
complement was rounded out by the appointment of another *bleu*,
Josselin le Corre, who, like Duclos-Guyot, had extensive experience
as a seaman in merchant as well as naval vessels.

There were several other notable additions: three young men of
middle-class birth who had not had the preferment of a *gardes*
background, but who sailed in hopes of qualifying as *bleu* officers
on merit; a captain's clerk of notable writing skills, but distinguished by his loathing for the navy; a well-educated and diligent
surgeon who was responsible for the health of the expedition, and
who went on to later renown; a chaplain, remarkable for his near-
invisibility during the voyage; and the most socially significant
member of *La Boudeuse's* gentlemanly occupants, Charles Nicolas
Othon d'Orange et de Nassau-Siegen, Prince of Nassau.

The Prince of Nassau was in his mid twenties and had served in
the French army at the end of the Seven Years' War. Very much the
handsome and somewhat roguish example of a dissolute young
nobleman whose adventures in Parisian society — he seems to have
been, like Bougainville, a lover of Sophie Arnould — were running
him into penury, he had been introduced to Bougainville at dinner
by a relative, the Comte de Maurepas, a past minister of marine. As
John Dunmore relates:

> The two had a long conversation, rapidly estab-
> lished a firm friendship, and Bougainville readily

accepted the suggestion that the young man might join him on the expedition. He would sail at his own expense, but his family were delighted by the arrangement since it removed him from the frivolities of French society and the possibility of incurring further debts. Bougainville had few occasions to regret his presence on board: he was far more helpful and companionable than demanding.[9]

The young prince would prove particularly adept at dealing with islanders with sensitivity and intelligence, which proved of great value to the expedition.

There was another, almost poignant appointment to *La Boudeuse* in the form of fifteen-year-old François-Guillaume de Vienne, who would serve as a seaman but would be considered an "irregular," or officer in training. He was the son of Madame de Vienne, in whose arms Bougainville possibly lay on the night before the Plains of Abraham battle in September 1759.[10]

To command the *Étoile*, Bougainville had the doughty, battle-scarred figure of François-Chenard de la Giraudais, the hardy seaman a few years older than Bougainville who had served aboard fishing vessels, privateers and merchantmen and who had an unparalleled record of fighting the British in the War of 1739–48 and the Seven Years' War. Emerging with a hero's record after the Treaty of Paris in 1763 and a *bleu* commission as a *lieutenant de frégate*, he nonetheless found his career blocked by the *rouges* and was glad to command *Sphinx* on the first Malouines voyage and *Étoile* on the second. His command of *Étoile* during the circumnavigation would finally lead to the reward of a permanent commission in the navy. Supporting Giraudais was his *seconde*, Jean-Louis Caro, who would keep an eloquent journal of the voyage, and a clutch of officers, mostly of *bleu* background, as well as a competent surgeon and a chaplain who would pay for his excessive behaviour ashore by being murdered in the street in Rio de Janeiro.

More significantly for the voyage, for European awareness of the discoveries that were about to be made and the advancement of science in general, were the scientific appointments made to *Étoile*. The naturalist for the voyage was to be Philibert Commerson. He was a year or two older than Bougainville, came from a similar legal family, and had early devoted himself to the study of botany while pursuing a medical degree. Having written several studies that earned him notice, he had moved to Paris on the death of his wealthy wife, where he became active with the community of naturalists in that city. They advised him to apply for the voyage, and upon meeting him Bougainville agreed to his appointment as "royal botanist and naturalist." Commerson was allowed to bring his own valet, who in the course of the expedition enlivened the voyage by being unmasked as Jeanne Baret, Commerson's mistress. Baret, who had masqueraded as a man, would survive the surprise of Bougainville and the crew, an attempted abduction by fascinated Tahitians, and the perils of the voyage to end her days as a pensioned tavern keeper, having earned a place in history as the first Frenchwoman to sail around the globe.

During the voyage, Commerson devoted himself diligently enough to the collection of natural specimens and he kept copious notes, although only in a rough and chaotic form that would not see print until a later century. More troubling was his personality, which was revealed as intolerant and waspish — deadly qualities for someone confined for years within a cramped sailing vessel. He dismissed *Étoile* as "that hellish den where hatred, insubordination, bad faith, brigandage, cruelty and all kinds of disorders reign." Commerson's dark, testy personality and the revelation of Baret's identity made Commerson unpopular with *Étoile*'s officers and men, and he was glad to leave the ship at Île de France (Mauritius) on the way home.[11]

At the other end of the personality spectrum was the expedition's astronomer, Pierre-Antoine Véron, seven years younger than Bougainville and from humble surroundings, where he had originally been trained to be a gardener. The support of a perceptive uncle helped to get him, on trial, into the School of Hydrography (France maintained one, but Britain did not), and from there, his quiet, gentle excellence won him entrance into the Paris Royal College, as well as the patronage of the noted mathematician Lalande. With Lalande's help, Véron had sailed on three previous voyages in naval vessels as astronomer/navigator, and was one of the few Western astronomers able to calculate longitude by the complex and difficult lunar observation method. His presence on the voyage added to Bougainville's own expertise and provided a superior degree of navigational skill: the expedition would at least have a clear idea of the navigational coordinates of any obstacle they might blunder into. This expertise accounted, in the end, as much as the seamanship of Duclos-Guyot and Giraudais, for the survival of the ships over so risky and lengthy a voyage.

The third member of the expedition's scientific contingent was the engineer/cartographer Charles Routier de Romainville, who was also in his early twenties and had served as an engineer officer in the army. He had been provided to Bougainville's first Malouines expedition as engineer/cartographer, and had remained in the settlement at Fort St-Louis until *La Boudeuse* arrived for the turnover ceremony to the Spanish. The latter were so impressed with de Romainville's work that they had offered him a captaincy in the Spanish service, but he instead accepted Bougainville's invitation to join the expedition. He would produce a superb folio of charts and artistic renderings, a large proportion of which, sadly, have not survived to the modern day. Like Véron, he was to leave the expedition in the Indian Ocean, at Île de France.[12]

If the king and the minister of marine had decide Bougainville should embark on the circumnavigation, they were in fact merely giving voice to a proposal he had begun drafting during the inactivity of his parole of 1760–61. Bougainville's ideas had been forming since before the war, and had been at first simply to seek that land Bouvet de Lozier had claimed to have found in 1739. But it had been his stay in London that first exposed him to the greater potential of the South Pacific, as he learned of English interest in the region based on Anson's 1740–44 voyage. The Spanish had protested the Falkland settlement, making it clear that any French designs on directly encroaching upon what the Spanish perceived as their territory — Bougainville had even briefly proposed a French settlement in California — was out of the question. In the hot summer weather, he again journeyed on horseback to Spain to conclude details of the Fort St-Louis handover, and the new plan became firm in his mind as he rode. As Dunmore relates:

> he consequently drafted out a new proposal as soon as his return from Madrid on October 16, 1766. The first stage of the voyage would be the handing over of the Malouines settlement to the Spanish, after which he would sail into the Pacific, either through the Straits of Magellan or by Cape Horn, and would survey "as much of and as best he will be able to, the lands lying between the Indies and the western coast of America, various parts of which have been sighted by navigators and named Diemen's Land, New Holland, Carpentaria, Land of the Holy Ghost, New Guinea, etc." After this, he would sail to China, with a possible call at the Philippines, and endeavour to find some island within reach of the China coast that could enable the French [East] India Company to trade …with China.[13]

The actual order finally issued to him gave Bougainville clear authority to claim any territories found for France, and particularly to look in the area where any temperate *Terra Australis* might lie.

> [A]s no European nation has any establishment or claim over these lands, it can only be in France's interest to survey them and take possession of them should they offer items useful to her trade and her navigation. With this in mind, the area that M. de Bougainville must concentrate on examining is especially the one stretching from the fortieth degree of southern latitude toward the

north, surveying what may lie between the two tropics.[14]

Even as the work of readying *La Boudeuse*, refitting *Étoile* and securing the expedition's supplies was going as well as he might have hoped, the summer of 1766 had not proven an easy one, in political or administrative terms. In the rushed few weeks after his return from Madrid, he dealt not only with the supportive Choiseul, who had moved on to another ministry in the peripatetic manner of the Louis XV government, but also with the new minister of marine, the Duc de Praslin. De Praslin placed a dismaying block on Bougainville's freedom of action by ordering him to return to France no later than early 1769. There was a fear of war with Britain in that year, and the government wanted Bougainville and his ships at home. Thus, not only would the expedition be delayed by however long it took to turn over the Fort St-Louis colony to the Spanish, but he was now bound to return within two years of leaving France, not the three that a detailed survey likely would require. Already the expedition was beginning to assume the form of a dash around the globe rather than a thoughtful progression.

In addition, there was a renewed Spanish hostility toward the expedition. Bougainville had, with characteristic openness, shown his orders to the Spanish ambassador, the Count de Fuentes, who was only now calming down over Bougainville's efforts to colonize the Malouines. His eyebrows shot up once again as he saw a renewed French effort to insert itself into a world that Spain considered, rather impractically but with great emotion, to be Spanish. De Fuentes announced he would have to seek Madrid's reaction to Bougainville's plan, which was unlikely to be positive. Choiseul, who was now foreign minister, received de Fuentes' stiff note and called Bougainville in to tell him to complete his preparations and get under way before a reply came from Madrid — one to which Choiseul and the king would have to respond. In a final lather, Bougainville cleared up his remaining obligations and was out of Paris by October 25. *La Boudeuse* finally sailed on the great adventure on November 15, 1766, Choiseul's urgency sending it off without the customary sea trials. *Étoile* was still being prepared at Rochefort, its sailing date still uncertain, but was ordered to join *La Boudeuse* at either Fort St-Louis or the South American mainland at Rio de Janeiro.

The always challenging conditions of the Bay of Biscay revealed flaws in *La Boudeuse's* hull and rig which the sea trials were designed to uncover. Two days out, a gale caused serious damage to its masts and spars, sending the main topmast and topgallant mast to the deck, cracking the remainder of the mainmast, and putting cracks in the lower foremast as well. Several sails were blown out of their boltropes, and all of this convinced Bougainville that the frigate was in no way ready for the storms of the great Southern Ocean and Cape Horn. Under a jury rig, Bougainville steered for Brest, where he ordered repairs and alterations to the ship's rig and hull. To reduce the top-hamper aloft, he had *La Boudeuse's* masts and yards shortened and reduced the sail area. In addition to recaulking the hull, he had the ship's twelve-pound guns exchanged for eight-pounders, reducing the burden on the hull and freeing more tonnage for equipment and supplies. The changes were effective, and by December 5 the industrious yardmen had finished their work. *La Boudeuse* punched out into the winter gales of the North Atlantic and began to fight its way south toward the sun.

Bougainville had had misgivings about the wisdom of using a fast warship design, essentially a gunnery platform, for a voyage of exploration. He had sought permission to move himself and the expedition's key personnel into the more prosaic *Étoile* for the voyage, if circumstances warranted. The minister wrote back in an understanding mood, before *La Boudeuse* cleared Brest:

> You will be the master, sir, of the decision whether
> to continue your expedition in accordance with
> what has been planned with the two ships the king
> has entrusted to your command or to send back
> the frigate *Boudeuse* if you do not consider she is

suitable for the purpose intended. H. M. leaves it to your prudence in this matter and leaves you free to continue on your way with both vessels or simply with one of them by choosing whichever will suit you best.[15]

The rigging and stowage changes Bougainville had made to the frigate would prove to have made its serviceable and a good sailer in open-ocean long passage conditions. The waters of Cape Horn or the Straits of Magellan might be another matter.

The passage south was uneventful, and on arrival at Montevideo on January 31, 1767, Bougainville found two Spanish frigates that were to take part in the transfer ceremony already riding at anchor. Both there and at Buenos Aires, Bougainville found the Spanish to be willing and helpful: the stores were replenished, the social welcome ashore was fulsome, and the only remaining worry was the fate of *Étoile* and how long it would be delayed at Rochefort. After three weeks, Bougainville and the Spanish sailed for the Malouines, Bougainville writing to Praslin before departure, "It will be en route to the Malouines that I shall test the frigate; the seas are heavy enough."[16]

As Bougainville predicted, the voyage to Fort St-Louis was a twenty-three-day battle against mountainous seas and heavy gales in which the shortened rig and improved stability of the hull brought *La Boudeuse* through with only moderate damage, but raised some concern as to the quality of its construction; Bougainville reported in his journal that, even before the heavier weather appeared, "… the outer end of the bowsprit broke off, even though the sea was fine and the wind moderate. The wood was not worth anything: unfortunately, I have to say the same thing about a good part of this frigate's materials."[17]

On arrival at Fort St-Louis, Bougainville found the colonists worried about British attacks. They had been visited by a warship promising eviction from what was deemed a British possession. The news of the transfer to Spanish authority was received glumly, but accepted, and thirty-seven colonists indicated they would

stay under Spanish rule for the short term. Bougainville found fifteen recruits for *La Boudeuse* among the men of the colony, and
finally, on April 1, 1767, the formal transfer took place, bringing
an end to Bougainville's dream of a French foothold at the gateway
to the Pacific. He had tried to provide a new future for the Acadian
refugees, but politics had also ended that. De Nerville, for his part,
declined the greater adventure of the circumnavigation, and would
return to France.

As Dunmore relates, there was a poignant quality to
Bougainville's last days in the Malouines:

> The Spanish frigates [with colonists aboard] left
> on April 27, Bougainville waiting for the *Étoile*
> which, according to the original plan, was to have
> joined the *Boudeuse* at the Malouines. He waited
> through May, making a few excursions around the
> islands for which he had harboured such hopes
> and which he was about to leave forever.... Then,
> on June 1, he weighed anchor. The *Étoile*, mean-
> while, had completed a difficult crossing to
> Montevideo, where she arrived at the beginning of
> May. Eventually receiving orders through the
> intermediary of the two Spanish frigates to pro-
> ceed to Rio de Janeiro, [it] arrived at Rio on June
> 13. The two ships finally came together there a
> week later.[18]

If Bougainville thought his circumstances had brightened
by a successful reunion with *Étoile* in the beautiful and bustling
port of Rio, he was mistaken. The viceroy, António Álvares da
Cunha, proved difficult to deal with, alternating between hospitality and cold hostility, the latter particularly after
Bougainville had sent carpenters to assist in repairing a nearby
Spanish vessel that had been all but quarantined by the viceroy.
The Spanish and Portuguese colonies in the Americas were virtually in a state of war, it seemed, and rather than a pleasant

respite before pushing on to Montevideo once again for the lengthier preparations for Cape Horn or the Straits, the Rio stay proved fraught with tension. *Étoile*'s chaplain had been murdered, with little likelihood of redress of the crime, and after a succession of disappointments and the viceroy's refusals to allow the purchase of timber, the rental of a shore house, or even the fair purchase of a small sloop to add to the French flotilla, matters came almost to blows:

> I was anxious [wrote Bougainville] to make a few representations to him on this subject, and also in regard to the purchase of the sloop and the wood; but he did not give me the chance, and ordered me out. Piqued no doubt by the fact that in spite of his rage I, as well as the officers accompanying me, remained seated, he called in his guard; but the guard, wiser than he, failed to appear.[19]

Bougainville determined to press southward earlier; the Spanish, if not as well-equipped as the Portuguese, might be more hospitable. On July 15, 1767, *La Boudeuse* and *Étoile* sailed, pointedly omitting to fire a salute to the viceroy. The feelings of the French were mixed: the place had been beautiful, the flora and fauna overwhelming in its abundance to Commerson. Bougainville expressed this ambivalence:

> During our stay at Rio de Janeiro we enjoyed the springtime of the poets. The view of this bay must always afford to travellers an intensity of pleasure.... Nothing could be finer than the views of the countryside that greet the eye whatever way one turns; and we should have been glad indeed to have seen more of this charming country. Its inhabitants had expressed to us in the frankest way the displeasure that they felt at the unfriendly treatment n ted out to us by their Viceroy, while for our part we were

only sorry that we were not able to remain for a longer time among them.[20]

On July 31, the flotilla arrived off Montevideo, where Bougainville had planned to stay no more than six weeks, readying for the Southern Ocean. But again, bad luck dogged the expedition. *Étoile* was rammed by a Spanish vessel, and as Montevideo offered no suitable yard to carry out the repairs, the ship had to be escorted by local vessels up the Rîo de la Plata to a shipyard at Ensenada de Barragán ("a bad port," Bougainville muttered, "inhabited by people who know no other happiness than idleness"). In getting there, Bougainville had taken over the pilotage up the narrow and shifting channel after the Spanish pilots had proven ignorant and incapable of keeping even their own craft off sandbanks. Here, the repairs would delay the departure for no less than three and a half months. There could be no question now of braving the horrors of the open-ocean passage to windward around Cape Horn. The expedition would attempt the tortuous route of the Straits of Magellan instead.[21]

Leaving the damaged and leaking *Étoile* in the hands of the somnolent Spanish carpenters and several exasperated French at Ensenada, Bougainville took one of the Spanish escort vessels — again, navigating himself — back to Montevideo and *La Boudeuse*. He went ashore to find the Spanish officials welcoming and accommodating, if not given to alacrity in any activity. He secured quarters that would allow him to send ashore a third of his crewmen at a time to enjoy the freedom of the town, on a rotating basis. Upon learning of the accident to *Étoile*, Bucarelli, the governor at Buenos Aires, had sent down to Bougainville two cargo boats to hold *Étoile*'s gear and stores while the work went on, and a small schooner to allow Bougainville to beat upriver to Ensenada from time to time to see how the work was progressing. The French carpenter's mates who had been left at Ensenada had galvanized the Spanish workmen, and the repairs had gone far more quickly than expected. Within three weeks, *Étoile* was afloat, re-rigged and ready to take on its stores and gear from the cargo boats. Delighted, Bougainville kept to his decision as to the expedition's route: there would be no challenge of Cape Horn.

The colonial government's aid was occasionally tempered by Spanish preoccupation with a social crisis of sorts. Following the French example, the Spanish were in the process of expelling the Jesuit order from their colonies, and the bitterness and disruption this caused had prevented many of the Acadian settlers of Fort St-Louis from getting passage to Europe on Spanish ships, as agreed. Bougainville did what he could for these discomfited refugees, and fretted over the sluggishness of the completion of *Étoile*'s reloading. He had time to reflect on the condition of the native population he had met, who toiled at the bottom of the colonial social ladder. What he saw did not inspire him:

> They struck me [he wrote] as being of an indolent nature; and they had, I noticed, that stupid expression which is so typical of trapped animals.[22]

The contrast between these downtrodden Guarani and the powerful Iroquois of North America must have been marked in his mind; yet no comparison appears in his writings.

Étoile finally was freed of the heat and mudflats at Ensenada on October 30, and the ship made the perilous passage through the unbuoyed sandbanks of the Rio de la Plata toward Montevideo. Still, ill luck dogged it: coming about quickly, with its ship's boat close under the bows sounding the channel, *Étoile* ran over the boat, drowning three men and necessitating an anchorage while the boat was raised. Then, as the passage continued, *Étoile* began to leak again. Exasperated, he anchored both ships in shallow water, and as the tide receded, Bougainville ordered a furious recaulking of as much of *Étoile*'s hull as could be reached and had *La Boudeuse* recaulked from the waterline up. Another gift arrived from the helpful Bucarelli in the form of a last-minute schooner-load of flour, which necessitated a restowage of the ships' supplies, and Bougainville put a final effort into securing any additional foodstuffs ashore, living or not, that could be barrelled, baled or herded to the ships in pursuit of his goal of ten months' self-sufficiency in supplies. At last, on November 14, 1767, the hands moved to the halyards on board *La Boudeuse* and *Étoile*, all plain sail was hoisted before a fair wind that inched the heavily laden vessels off over sandbanks revealed by an exceptionally low tide, and then they were riding free in the ebb on the great estuary, turning southward into the South Atlantic, bound for the Pacific. A full year had passed since *La Boudeuse* had sailed from France, and it had little more than a year to complete a voyage meant to circle the globe and find what it could in the vast South Pacific. It was precious little time for such an undertaking.[23]

As the Uruguayan coastline receded astern, Bougainville had time to reflect more thoughtfully on the native population and its plight. He observed, with a perceptive pity:

> One may see ... that the Indians possessed no individual property of any kind, and that they were subjected to a cruelly tedious routine of work and play. This ennui, so rightly called "mortal," is explanation enough of the well-known fact that they passed out of this life without regret, and died without ever having really lived. When once they fell ill, it was but rarely they recovered, and when asked if they looked on death as a misfortune, they answered "no," and answered it with a conviction that left no doubt of their sincerity.... For the rest, the Jesuits represented these Indians to us as a race incapable of attaining a higher degree of intelligence than that of children, and the lives these big children led prevented them from sharing the gaiety of little ones.[24]

The passage south toward the strait gradually worsened, and in a series of powerful storms, Bougainville lost all his livestock, who died in their pens due to the violence of the ships' motions. Grimly the ships fought on, in what had been supposed to be the most clement period of weather, the southern summer. Finally, the prominent mark of land that announced entrance to the strait, the Cape of Virgins, came into view. Bougainville recorded the sighting in his log:

> Friday 4 [December] to Saturday 5. Full moon the 5th at 2.12 pm. Winds: SW to WNW, storm. High winds, heavy seas, hove to under foresail and mizzen. At 1 o'clock the foresail tore, we reefed it and ran under bare poles. The lead having given us only 20 fathoms, grey sand, red gravel and shells, the fear of the breakers that stretch out to the SSE of Cape of Virgins decided me to remain under bare poles, all the more because this enabled us to replace the foresail. At 4 we set out on the port tack with the main and mizzen staysails. At 7 o'clock set the courses; at midnight changed tack until 3. At 6 a.m. the wind died down, trimmed the sails, at 8 we tacked.
>
> Run at a rough estimate for the 24 hours N x NE 2° E, 37'. I reckon that I am 9 to 10 leagues WNW from the Cape of Virgins. Observed latitude 51° 51'. Corrected longtitude 70° 25' 30".[25]

It took another two days of exhausting tacking and constant sounding to work the ships into the open approaches of the Strait, marked now by the grim rock of the Cape of Virgins on one side and Cape Possession on the other. It took continuing extreme care and labour to work the ships toward the first narrows, where any period of anchoring would be possible. The anchor was dropped from time to time to allow assessment of the next tack to steer as they felt their way in, guided by uncertain charts, the stone ramparts of the shores looming frighteningly close at each turn. Now they were beginning to attract attention ashore, from Patagonian natives to the north and Tierra del Fuegans to the south:

At 8 a.m. the Patagonians raised a white flag near the Narrows, no doubt the same one that M. de la Giraudais [in *Étoile*] had given them in June, 1766. We answered by raising the ship's ensign. The savages of Tierre de Fuego also came, numbering approximately 20, on the port side as you enter the Narrows. They were on foot and dressed in skins. They followed us and gestured as though calling us.[26]

Finally, shelter was found:

Tuesday 8 [December] to Wednesday 9. At midday, being inside the pass, we let out the topsails, set the courses and steered WSW. At a $1/4$ past midday 34 fathoms rocky bottom, at 12.45 15 fathoms rocky bottom, a few minutes later 14 fathoms, same ground. Sighted Cape Gregory bearing SW x W. At 2.45 with a slack tide and almost calm, we anchored in 18 fathoms mud about $1^1/2$ leagues from land.[27]

This welcome anchorage, in what would later be known as Boucault Bay, marked the end of the first part of the voyage. *La Boudeuse* and *Étoile* had made the long sweep down the east coast of South America and battled headwinds and huge seas to work doggedly into the mountainous, forbidding entrance to the strait. Now they were in, and they could gather their strength for the challenging passage of the tortuous, winding strait to the Pacific Ocean. The ships rode to their anchors between the fjordlike walls of some of the most inhospitable lands on earth. Soon after, however, Bougainville ordered boats to be lowered from both vessels, and they rowed ashore, to be greeted by an enthusiastic shore party of Patagonians:

As soon as we had anchored, I lowered a boat and signalled the *Étoile* to do the same. We landed opposite the ships…. Hardly had we walked a few steps when we saw some savages, 6 in number, racing toward us on horseback. They dismounted at 60 paces and gaily and confidently marched toward us, shouting *chaoua, chaoua.* We made a great fuss of them; in the two hours we spent ashore their number grew to thirty. I had bread and biscuit given to them. This group is the same as the one seen in 1766 by the *Aigle* and the *Étoile.* They were extremely welcoming in their gestures, clutching us in their arms and expressing the greatest joy in seeing us.[28]

The Patagonians were not, however, the giants of sailors' legends.

So such are these Patagonians whom some travellers described to us as giants, and whom in 1765 the English on M. Byron's ships reported as giants…. These men are of a good height, but the tallest one I met attained scarcely a height of 5 ft. 9 in. Several were of my height, and thanks be to God I am only 5 feet 6 in.[29]

It is likely that Bougainville had been recognized by the Patagonians from his own earlier visit in March of 1766, when he had distributed presents. "I went back to see the Savages," he had then written, "… their number had increased. I gave them blankets, shirts, hoods, belts, coppers and pans, axes, handles, knives, mirrors and some cinnibar."[30] His largesse then, and the civility of his people, largely explained the welcome. He observed them with the care he had brought to the observation of the North American warrior societies, and noticed that there appeared to be no hierarchical structure to their society:

I believe that no single one of them was possessed individually of any more influence than the other…. I believe these people live the same life as Tartars, wandering over the immense plains of South America, always in the saddle, men, women, and children alike.[31]

The greater concern of the successful passage of the strait now confronted Bougainville. The two ships had a distance of 375 miles to transit before they reached the waters of the South Pacific, through a fjordlike body that varied between 12 and 20 miles in width, with powerful currents and a prevailing headwind out of the west against which the ships had to tack — or anchor, when possible, to await a favourable wind. It would take Bougainville fifty-two exhausting and strenuous days to make the transit, the ships beset with peril at all times in a near-arctic environment that tried the endurance of commander and crews alike.

The constant manoeuvring in the face of headwinds and against the fluctuating currents, in waters where the soundings were uncertain, and off the most inhospitable of barren, windswept rocky shores, had revealed the strengths and weaknesses of *Étoile* and *La Boudeuse*:

> Saturday, [January] 16. I cannot but renew my complaints about the kind of vessel supplied for such a voyage. It could not be less suitable. On her own, the *Étoile* would have cleared the strait long ago…. The *Étoile*, a better sailer than we are, offers a quarter more to the wind and drifts a quarter less. This unfortunate frigate cannot tack without losing a great deal of ground. In truth, we could not have a less effective means of transport…. God save us from greater misadventures in this *Boudeuse*.[32]

Day after gruelling day the passage went on. The ships halted at Bougainville Bay to allow wood to be cut, and *La Boudeuse* was "boot-topped," which meant heeling it over enough to scrape off the line of weed that had built up along the waterline, a task that slowed it. More natives came, this time from the wilder Tierra del Fuego side, to challenge any remaining notions Bougainville might have had about the nobility of humanity when found in a simpler state.

> We had a visit on board from several native canoes. They belong to the Pecherais group, small, ugly, knock-kneed and the most wretched of men.... They go naked, wearing nothing more than a scruffy skin that can hardly cover them. To be frank, when one sees these savages, however much one would like to philosophize, one could not express any preference for man in that state of nature over civilized man.[33]

The passage wore on, with innumerable incidents: *Étoile* sprang a leak again, which was found from within the hull and successfully stopped; Commerson got ashore with Véron and made observations and collected specimens; de Romainville worked diligently on a reliable chart of the strait. Although it was summer, the weather continued in wintry gloom and storm:

> Tuesday [January] 19. New moon at 6h 20' 45" a.m. High wind from the SW to WNW with rain and the usual gusts. I was affected by a severe sore throat for which I was bled three times. Several of our men also affected. If one did not die of sickness in this cursed climate one would die of impatience and boredom.[34]

There were endless, exhausting challenges to the nautical skills of both crews:

> Friday [January] 22. At 2 p.m. the NNW winds shifted to SSW with such fury that one could not look into the wind. Hail came with this storm

which was the wildest I have ever experienced in my life. We had to drop a second anchor and keep our large anchor in a state of readiness. We dragged, as did *Étoile*. Our mizzen sail tore loose and we had to lower the yard in order to save what was left of it. We raised our second anchor as soon as the weather returned to normal. Throughout the day, stormy gale from WSW to WNW with squalls and rain. We struck our yards and topmasts.[35]

Finally, on Tuesday, January 26, 1768, Bougainville was able to make the following entry:

Bearings at 2 o'clock: Cape Victories NW 8 leagues; Cape Pillars S 3°W, 2 leagues. These bearings enabled me to determine the ... latitudes and longtitudes of Cape Pillars and Cape Victories. From 2.30 until 8 o'clock, we followed various tacks, and the winds variable W to WNW then N fresh breeze, all sails set to round the land. Bearings at 6 o'clock: Cape Victories NW, the most W island of the Evangelists WNW 4°W, Cape Pillars S x SE 3°S. At 7 o'clock we had rounded Cape Pillars.[36]

The expedition had passed the westernmost point of the last obstacle, now known as Cabo Pilar on the Isla Desolación. *La Boudeuse* and *Étoile* were in the open vastness of the Pacific Ocean. Bougainville carefully observed his starting point for the great crossing that lay ahead:

I am taking my point of departure from the above bearings on Bellin's map and following that map in latitude 52° 58' and longitude 77° 44' [west of the] Paris meridian. [After observation] my true point of departure being as above in latitude 52° 50' S, longitude 79° 9' west of Paris.[37]

By nightfall of the next day, the snow-capped peaks of South America's mountains seemed to have sunken into the sea astern. Ahead, still almost halfway around the world, lay the East Indies.

For three weeks, the two ships pitched slowly northwestward, spreading apart during the day until only the topgallants were visible to see about them as widely as possible, then converging to sail closer together during the night, when the small yellow glow of the stern lanterns provided comfort and company in the huge emptiness of the sea. At first the ships tacked into the frigid westerlies, shouldering into the grey seas and ominous swells of the Southern Ocean as the watchmen stamped and shivered on deck. But gradually the heavy seas abated, the air warmed, and finally the winds shifted astern as *La Boudeuse* and *Étoile* crossed into the realm of the southeast trade winds. The sea became deep blue, flecked with brilliant whitecaps, and the air lost its chill. The sky changed to a brilliant, crystalline blue, across which orderly rows of clouds drifted before the steady winds. All sheets were hauled aft, and the topgallants and topsails did their still, steady work in great curves of silent power ahead of the constant southeasterlies. The changes of the watch came with a *ting* of the bell, the turn of the hourglass, and a few murmured words between officers and men as the helmsmen simply held to the same course they had steered on the watch before — and indeed, the day before. Flying fish leaped away from the slowly plunging bows and their boiling white foam, and porpoises raced like green ghosts deep ahead of the bow wave or arced in exuberant flights, singly or in pairs, up and over the sun-dappled waves, to slip sleekly back again. The reef points tapped on the sunwashed surfaces of the sails, while the hull and rigging creaked rhythmically and steadily as the shadows cast by the forenoon sun moved slowly back and forth across the warm deck. The rush of the sea under the counter tumbled aft to leave a white trail of foam that stretched to the horizon, and in the lee of the longboat or in half a dozen other corners of the ship, men off watch curled in the open to sleep, the hammocks in the airless world below forgotten. It was the seaman's paradise, trade wind sailing, and as it passed, day after languorous day, the exhaustion and strain of the Magellan passage healed, faded and was forgotten.

The days were neither without incident, nor occasional bouts of stormy weather, when the trade winds briefly failed. Several crewmen began to display symptoms of scurvy, but were treated by the doctor and Bougainville with a regime of strict cleanliness and a diet supplemented by imaginative means:

> Since the 14th [of February] we have been continuing to catch enough fish to supply at least a third of the crew. This morning we rationed water to one *pot* per man per day of which half is for the boiler. Since we came out of the strait we have caught more than 200 rats. I am giving 3 *sols* for each one caught.[38]

A further month of sailing brought the ships to the eastern end of the great arc of low atolls that lie to the east of Tahiti ("Tuesday 22 [March]. At 6 a.m. the *Étoile* signalled the presence of four islands approximately to the SE and at the same moment we saw one to the W distant approximately 4 and a half leagues"[39]). Bougainville steered toward the island seen to the west, and to the seaworn crews its prospect was very appealing.

> The verdure charmed our eyes, and the cocoanut palms everywhere offered us their fruits and their shades adorned with flowers, while the thousands of birds fluttering about the shore revealed that there were plenty of fish; but, although we longed to go on shore, no anchorage could be found, and so, unhappily, we had to abandon the idea of landing.[40]

Bougainville's caution was also drawn to the appearance of some twenty islanders: tall, well-muscled men, wearing very little, who carried armfuls of long javelins and postured threateningly. The ships sheered away, and for the next week or two they found themselves amidst a sprawling group of low, often awash islets interspersed with unexpected reefs that on more than one occasion threatened to wreck the ships. Bougainville labelled the island chain with political deference as the Bourbon Archipelago, but described them personally as the "Dangerous Archipelago"; in modern times they would revert to the native name, the Tuamotus.

Finally, a different sort of sighting was made — not of yet another low, wave-washed atoll, but of substantial land:

> Friday 1 [April] to Saturday 2. Full moon on the 2nd at 8.05 a.m.... At 10.30 a.m we saw two extremely high lands, namely one islet in the shape of an isolated peak, which I am naming *Le Boudoir* [the island of Mehetia, east of Tahiti] bearing NNE 5° E distant about 5 leagues, and a larger stretch of land equally high bearing W x NW and WNW, distant approximately 14 to 15 leagues.[41]

This was Bougainville's first sighting of the island of Tahiti, and he was only the second European commander to make it, having been preceded by a few months by the British Captain Samuel Wallis aboard HMS *Swallow*. The approach to the island proved difficult, given the set of currents and the limitations of the ships, which now had to contend with squally weather, rain and variable winds. But as they closed with the island, the Europeans realized with astonishment that they were arriving at a very different place:

> During the afternoon [March 4] we stood in for the land. The whole coast rises in an amphitheatre with deep gullies and high mountains. Part of the land seems to be cultivated, the rest is wooded. Along the sea, at the foot of the high country, runs a band of low land, covered with trees and habitations, and as a whole, this island presents a charming aspect. Over a hundred canoes, of various

sizes, but all with outriggers, came around the
ships…. We have to windward a fine waterfall
coming down from the mountaintop that makes
your mouth water. There is a village at the foot of
it, in the shadow of an orchard of trees. The sea
does not appear to break along the coast in this
part, we shall try to anchor there. At 11, I signalled the *Étoile* to lower a boat.[42]

It took until March 6 for careful soundings to reveal a pass —
now called Boudeuse Pass — through the inshore reef, into which
the two ships carefully steered, coming to anchor off the village of
Hitia'a, on the east coast of Tahiti Nui, or Greater Tahiti, which
was the larger portion of the dumbbell-shaped island. The anchorage would prove not as sheltered, nor with as good a holding
ground, as Bougainville had hoped — both ships would lose
ground tackle there, and *La Boudeuse* more than one anchor —
but the ships would remain there until they sailed on April 15,
1768. They would carry away a Tahitian passenger and an
astounded Bougainville, whose account of what he believed he had
found would stun, dismay and inspire European intellectual
thought in this most revolutionary of centuries and create an
image of terrestrial paradise that continues to this day. The revelation of Tahiti, and the European reaction to Bougainville's
accounts, will be examined in the next chapter.

After a stay that could only be described at restorative to the
crews of both ships, *La Boudeuse* and *Étoile* sailed westward again on
April 15, narrowly escaping wrecking on Tahiti's reefs as they did so.
The stay had been costly in terms of equipment, as *La Boudeuse* had
lost no fewer than two large anchors and four kedge anchors trying
to maintain the anchorage at Hitia'a. But the beneficial effects of the
stay on the crews, and on the question of supplies, had been marked.

Between what has been used during the stay by the
two ships and what has been taken on board in the
way of refreshments, we obtained through barter

800 heads of poultry and close on 150 pigs. Without the troublesome tasks of the last few days, we could have obtained far more because the Indians were bringing more than ever. The sick found much relief on land during their brief stay here. The air in this island is most salubrious and, once the good anchorage was identified, it would be one of the best places of call in the world.[43]

It would be another five weeks of westward sailing before the French set foot on land again. Their course took them through the Society Islands, then through the southern part of the Samoan Group, where the islanders, similar in appearance and culture to the Tahitians, had little interest in trade and displayed an armed apprehension rather than welcome. The expedition sailed on without landing.

Bougainville now had to confront the rising incidence of scurvy in his crews, as the fresh foodstuffs obtained at Tahiti had been devoured and the men had to rely on the "hard rations" of salted meat, dried peas and granitic biscuit that had been packed in France. The poor charts at his disposal made Bougainville wary of closing with the land — he had few anchors left to spare — but the acute need for replenishment ashore finally could not be denied. Entering the island group that he named the Great Cyclades, and which James Cook would soon title the New Hebrides (now Vanuatu), Bougainville brought the ships to anchor off the small island of Aoba, between Espiritu Santo and Pentecost. The former island had been seen in 1606 by the Portuguese explorer de Quirós, who had mistaken it for the tip of the Great South Land. Bougainville's arrival disproved that theory, and Véron's invaluable observations fixed the latitude and longitude of the island group accurately. Again, the population proved by no means as appealing to the French as the Tahitians.

The people are ugly, short in stature, [and] covered in leprosy. They are naked except for the natural

parts. A few have painted chests. They are of two
colours, black and mulatto. They have frizzy hair
and thick lips, they pierce their nostrils to hang a
few ornaments. I did not see any with a beard.[44]

From Vanuatu, an unappreciative Bougainville steered directly
west, hoping to confirm the existence or absence of New Holland,
which had been sighted and named by the Dutch. The ships
crossed the Coral Sea without incident, passing unknowingly just
north of the treacherous Diane Bank, but then closed with the
Great Barrier Reef of Australia. Through the vigilance of the lookouts, a disaster was averted.

Monday 6 [June] to Tuesday 7. Continuation of
the fresh ESE to SE winds. I was steering W x SW
when at half past one we became aware of breakers
ahead, approximately 2 miles from the W x SW to
WNW...We changed tack immediately and we
steered NNE altering around until we had returned
to W and then W x SW. These breakers covered a
wide extent with several rocks visible above the
water. Some people thought they could see a low
land SW of the breakers. From 4 o'clock we had
reverted to the W x SW course when at 5.30 they
shouted from aloft that they could see new breakers about 5 miles away from WSW to NNW with
a fair number of uncovered rocks, a third warning
to me not to insist on seeking land along this parallel.... The encounter with this succession of
breakers does not allow me to continue to seek
Quiros' southern continent here.[45]

At this reef, now known as Bougainville Reef, Bougainville
turned away from what could have been a French discovery of the
east coast of Australia, leaving it to James Cook to coast and claim
for Britain. Yet it is possible that his lookouts had seen the land,

and, had entry into the maze of reefs been possible, the history of modern Australia might have been quite different.

Bougainville now turned the expedition north. Uncertain of the passage between New Guinea and whatever might lie to the south of it, Bougainville closed with the New Guinea coast, but then determined to tack *eastward* around its easternmost headland, to then sail north around it in a huge arc to reach the East Indies — modern day Indonesia — where Dutch trading stations were located and supplies might be obtainable. The New Guinea natives they encountered along the coast were not welcoming. "They were armed with bows, arrows and spears, they uttered great cries and it appeared to me that their attitude was not peaceful…. Where can one find men like the good [Tahitians]!"[46]

New Guinea was rounded, the northward course was resumed, and Bougainville now steered into the New Georgia group of islands, seeing ahead of him high land between which he would steer (through Bougainville Strait), naming the easternmost of the land masses Choiseul, after his mentor. The western one would eventually carry Bougainville's own name. To the entire group he bestowed the name Louisiades, but today they are known as the Solomon Islands. Once within this group, the ships anchored briefly off Choiseul, but then Bougainville steered northwest along the north coast of Bougainville Island, hesitating to anchor and risk attack from the islanders, whose few numbers he did see had behaved in anything but a welcoming manner. Finally, as *La Boudeuse* had almost exhausted its supply of firewood and fresh water, New Britain and New Ireland were seen ahead, and Bougainville selected the nearer one, New Ireland, for an anchorage.

In a drenching downpour, the ships came to anchor off a steaming, dark jungle shore that emitted clouds of mosquitos and seemed to the sodden, ragged crewmen who went ashore to be alive with alarming insect life and poisonous serpents. Fresh water was found, and there was wood in abundance, but no welcoming natives from whom fresh food could be bartered. The weather remained foul; it was now the rainy season, and day after day the ships were drowned in dark, cloaking downpours that rendered everything damp, mildewed and decaying. "We are in Hell," muttered Bougainville, as the health of both ships' crews began to deteriorate rapidly and they were still hundreds of leagues from any possible help. Véron's observations in the few clear moments had given them a definite idea of their location, those series of exacting navigational coordinates being one of the most significant legacies of the voyage. Bougainville despaired privately in his journal:

> I have been compelled once more to cut back the bread ration by one ounce, the little food we have is largely spoilt.... And when will it end? Such is our situation that we are suffering at the same time from the past that has weakened us, the present whose sad features are repeated time and time again and the future whose indeterminacy is the most cruel of our woes. My personal sufferings are multiplied by those of the others. Nonetheless I must make it known ... that courage outclasses misfortunes.[47]

With the scurvy cases worsening daily, Bougainville now realized that their survival depended upon reaching a European settlement, hopefully one of the Dutch East India Company posts in the Molucca group of islands off northwestern New Guinea. The expedition pressed on past the Admiralty Islands — Bougainville ordered the expedition's shore tents to be cut apart and made into clothing for the seamen, who were now virtually wearing mildewed rags — and then steered for the island of Buru, where Bougainville's charts told him a Dutch post had once stood. On September 1, 1768, to the tearful relief of all on board, *La Boudeuse* and *Étoile* rounded the headland of Buru and saw the infinitely cheering sight of the Dutch flag flying from a staff above a small stockaded fort and the tidy house of the Dutch resident, Hendrick Ouman. Ouman was kindly toward the emaciated French, providing a vast meal for all — "The Dutch were amazed at the voracity we displayed when eating. For my part, I declare that this supper was one of the most delicious moments of my life," recalled Bougainville. Ouman's suspicions about the purpose of Bougainville's expedition did not prevent him from aiding the French as best he could, helping with supplies and the care of the sick until Bougainville sailed on to Batavia (the modern Djakarta), the Dutch colonial capital. Bougainville made the passage, threading his way through innumerable islands over a distance of more than a thousand miles in twenty-two days with little incident. The voyage was made easier by the steady monsoon winds, a relative ease of navigation — there were few low-lying atolls — and the welcome friendliness of the islanders, who flocked alongside in their outriggers and handed up fruits, vegetables and almost anything the French needed, for low prices or easy barter. The worn and salt-stained ships pressed on until, on September 28, 1768, the roadstead before Batavia came abruptly into view, the shoreline marked by the unmistakable line of European rooftops. They had returned to the world of known sea routes and of European settlement. Bougainville's feelings were plain: "[We arrived] in one of the most beautiful colonies in the world, where we all considered our voyage to have ended."[48]

For all practical purposes, Bougainville had completed the unknown portion of his voyage, and was, remarkably, adhering to the restrictive timetable Praslin had set for him. There was little to show for the voyage in terms of new cartographic knowledge, other than the confirmation that, in the latitudes he had navigated, no Great South Land existed. He had corrected some misconceptions about Spanish or Portuguese discoveries of the 1600s in the western Pacific and named some new islands. But in scientific terms, the expedition's greatest achievement lay in the accuracy with which island groups' latitudes and longitudes, and the true scope of the Pacific, had been established by Véron's careful and precise astronomical observations. It was these observations, married to the later geographical discoveries of Britain's James Cook, that completed the basis of Europe's exploration and charting of the essential elements of the Pacific map. Bougainville had not found what he had secretly hoped to find: another New France in the Southern Ocean. But he had made, in the most socially significant experience of the voyage, an intense and meticulously recorded visit to the island of Tahiti, the record of which would impact on European thinking with an electric shock. It would remain, along with a South American flower Commerson had named for Bougainville, the most lasting legacy of the voyage.

The return voyage to France from Batavia would follow the known sailing routes of the Dutch, with one exception: it was Bougainville's intention to put in to Île de France in the Indian Ocean before attempting the final swing around the Cape of Good Hope and the long Atlantic passage up to France. He got away to sea as soon as he could, on October 16, 1768. He had been well supplied by the affable Dutch, albeit for good prices, but he sailed with a weakened and ailing crew: dysentery, bred in the sewage-choked Dutch canals of the otherwise charming Batavia, had begun to make inroads with his crew, as it would with James Cook's not long after. Once clear of the harbour, Bougainville ordered *Étoile* to make its own way to Port Louis, at Île de France. Embarking the most seriously ill aboard the faster *La Boudeuse*, Bougainville would race ahead. It was almost too late: on arrival twenty days later at Port Louis, fifty-five men were desperately ill, and the wardroom favourite, the Chevalier de Bouchage, died in Bougainville's arms. The frigate itself did not escape injury when the local pilot, to Bougainville's fury, drove it aground entering the Port Louis harbour, necessitating a further delay for repairs.[49]

With Praslin's deadline looming, Bougainville sought, and secured from the island's *intendant,* Poivre, support to repair the damage the grounding had done to the frigate's hull, as well as to secure the last load of supplies that would see them safely through to France. It was revealed that the expedition would lose its key scientists here: Commerson, Véron and de Romainville had accepted invitations to stay on Île de France to pursue other interests. *Étoile* had rolled in safely, but needed careening for hull cleaning and repairs to leaks that had begun again. It was decided that Bougainville would push on ahead in *La Boudeuse*, while *Étoile* would sail to France alone whenever it could.

On December 12, 1768, *La Boudeuse* cleared Port Louis's harbour and steered for the Cape of Good Hope. The Dutch there were welcoming and hospitable, but they surprised Bougainville with news that a British circumnavigating expedition was mere days ahead of them, in the form of a vessel about *Étoile*'s size carrying the Englishman Philip Carteret. Carteret's voyage had uncannily mirrored Bougainville's, and ashore in the rain-sodden gloom of New Ireland the French had found evidence of Carteret's passing: he had anchored in the same small bay that Bougainville had chosen, an extraordinary coincidence given the vastness of the Pacific and the myriad islands. Now Carteret's ship, the wallowing, weed-fouled *Swallow*, was just ahead. Bougainville remained at the Cape for eight days, where he was feted and supplied by the businesslike Dutch, and then sailed, pausing at Ascension Island to secure sea turtles before pressing northward. *La Boudeuse*'s mast and yards were weak, and the mainmast was cracked, requiring Bougainville to strike topgallants and sail only under topsails and courses. The frigate still managed a good turn of speed, and on February 25, 1769, it overhauled the plodding *Swallow*, boiling up from astern as if the English vessel was standing still. Bougainville spoke with Carteret, offering assistance, which was politely refused. Bougainville did not reveal that he, too, was returning from a circumnavigation, and he agreed to carry some mail for Carteret to Europe. *La Boudeuse* forged ahead, leaving Carteret astern "as if she lay at anchor. His ship was very small, went very ill ... how much he must have suffered in so bad a vessel may well be conceived," reflected Bougainville. Carteret's mastheads disappeared astern by nightfall. Passing the Azores on March 4, Bougainville was off the French coast by the fourteenth. His initial intention had been to make for Brest, but the always challenging Bay of Biscay weather intervened with a vicious squall that tore at the frigate's weakened rig, breaking the forecourse yard and doing so much damage to the disintegrating mainmast that Bougainville knew he needed downwind shelter, and soon. Putting up the helm, he ran before the wind for the shelter of St-Malo, where the grand Pacific dream had first been launched. On March 16, 1769, two years and four months after *La Boudeuse*'s departure from Nantes, the frigate dropped anchor in the harbour at St-Malo. It had lost only thirteen men in the long circumnavigation, a remarkable feat for the age.

The long voyage was over. Now would come the reaction to what Bougainville related he had seen. His first reports would not have the support of the observations of his scientists, still far astern on Île de France. He had not found sizeable new lands to colonize, nor had he opened a possible trade route with China or even found a new source of spices, all goals of the original expedition. But what he had in fact found, and would describe, would have impact nonetheless.

Chapter Seven

Paradise Found?
The Revelation of Tahiti

When Louis-Antoine de Bougainville first gazed upon the shores of Tahiti, he was not the first European navigator to have done so. That distinction went to Captain Samuel Wallis of the Royal Navy, commanding the frigate *Dolphin*, which had entered the Pacific Ocean in 1767 as part of a two-ship expedition sent by Britain to explore for the Great South Land. *Dolphin*'s consort had been the slow and crank *Swallow*, commanded by Philip Carteret, from which *Dolphin* became separated soon after exiting the Strait of Magellan. *Dolphin*, a copper-bottomed frigate of good speed, sailed on ahead to complete a circumnavigation of which the most important result was the finding of Tahiti, or "King George's Island," in the midst of the South Pacific. *Dolphin*'s return to England in time to impart the news of this discovery would give the impending voyage of Lieutenant James Cook, in the little collier *Endeavour*, a landfall to steer for. Carteret, in *Swallow*, would sail too far to the north and miss Tahiti, struggling on homeward at such as agonizingly slow pace that, as has been seen, Bougainville overhauled him in the South Atlantic.

Wallis had sailed with similar instructions to those of Bougainville, and he sailed much the same route, narrowly escaping disaster in the Tuamotus, and then, on June 18, 1767, sighting a high island to the west at sunset. The next morning revealed a towering, 7,000-foot island of awesome beauty, toward which Wallis now steered. As they approached, hundreds of outrigger canoes, filled with handsome people who seemed enthusiastically friendly, swarmed out to meet the ship. The mood of the natives changed as *Dolphin*, with its cutter sounding ahead of it, worked in toward the island in search of an anchorage, finally finding one in the beauty of what is now Matavai Bay, on June 23. Attacks by the islanders were replied to, first with musket fire, and finally by devastating broadsides from *Dolphin's* great guns, which, as the ship's sailing master George Robertson described, "struck such terror among the poor unhappy crowd that it would require the pen of Milton to describe...."[1]

The use of firepower and an evident willingness to kill convinced the Tahitians to attempt friendship rather than a suicidal confrontation, and a reasonably amicable relationship with Wallis' crew, which ripened into genuine liking, then followed. The English were granted free access to the island's bounty, including many of its attractive young women, and the departure five weeks later was filled with genuine regret on the part of *Dolphin's* young crew, and an apparently equal regret on the part of the agreeable islanders.

To see the place now is to imagine with little difficulty its impact on a land-starved eighteenth-century ship's crew, exhausted after a gruelling passage. Tahiti remains, as it was in 1767, an island of surpassing beauty. Its tall central mountains, two major peaks which are remnants of ancient volcanoes, fall away to the sea in fissured valleys and ridges covered in green verdure, down to coastal lands which are heavily treed in palm and marked here and there by exquisite waterfalls. Now as then the inhabitants live along the coastal plain, with only a few pockets of urban congestion; trees, lush flowers, gardens and beautiful "prospects" greet the eye at every turn and the lagoon is serene, while to seaward the surf roars distantly on the protecting reef. Only Rio de Janeiro approaches its green grandeur, and the beauty of the place remains in spite of colonial development, a huge airstrip and the coming of the modern age. Very little is left of the old Tahiti, but the trade winds still whisper in the graceful palms, the flowers bloom, and the scent of *monoi*, a coconut-sandalwood oil, worn by today's women as it was two hundred and fifty years ago as a dressing and fragrance for the hair and the body, still floats on the breeze amidst the exhaust fumes of scooters and diesel-powered buses. The impact of such an environment in its pristine state on eighteenth-century European crews — cramped, dirty and ill-fed after months of harsh seafaring — is not difficult to understand.

As Bougainville worked in to anchor within the reef, sounding carefully, the canoes of the islanders crowded around the ships once again:

> Tuesday 5 [April]. At 6 p.m.: the most N point bore W 5° S, the low headland W x SW; the first point of the fine bay S x E, the most S point SE x S. A great deal of bartering with the Savages who do not seem to be surprised to see us, and are skillful traders, but display good faith. A young and fine-looking girl came in one of the canoes, almost naked....[2]

For a few iron nails tossed down by a seaman from *La Boudeuse*, the girl cheerfully revealed the rest of her figure, which caused a general rush to the rail. Bougainville would later relate the event, with some classical allusions, in his published account of the voyage: "The young girl negligently allowed her loincloth to fall to the ground, and appeared to all eyes such as Venus showed herself to the Phrygian shepherd." It would contribute to the image of Tahiti as "New Cythera" — Bougainville's eventual name for Tahiti — a replicated paradise of the classical world.

By the next day, Bougainville's slow and cautious sounding of the treacherous lagoon within the reef finally produced what appeared to be a reasonable anchorage. The anchors went down, and *La Boudeuse* and *Étoile* had arrived in what seemed, for all intents and purposes, to be a version of Paradise.

> Wednesday 6 [April]. At 1.30 the *Étoile's* boat gave signal of a good anchorage facing a village and a small river inside the reefs and following a channel that separates them. I ordered a boat to lead the way

and we steered a course basing ourselves on the
Étoile's boat. At 2 o'clock we dropped anchor in 30
fathoms, bottom of grey sand, shells and gravel, and
Étoile anchored a quarter of an hour later. We let out
a kedge anchor secured to two cablets and hauled on
them to moor further inside the reefs. Moored SE
and NW and [struck] the lower yards and topmasts.
Bearings of the anchorage: its position: latitude 17°
33' S and longitude 150° 36' 17" west of Paris.[3]

If the islanders were welcoming, it was a cautious welcome —
Bougainville did not know of Wallis's free use of his guns, and *La
Boudeuse* presented a similarly ominous row of open gunports —
and the islanders would not let the French come freely ashore
until their length of stay had been negotiated. The leading men
held what Bougainville, with his memories of the Iroquois of
Oswegatchie, referred to as a "council," and he began to refer to
them as "Indians" rather than "Savages."

I explained that we were coming to sleep ashore in
order to obtain water and wood, and that for this I
needed 18 days, after which we would leave. I gave
him a number of stones equal to the number of
days I expected to stay. Deliberations of the council: they wanted to remove 9 stones, I did not agree.
In the end everything was settled, the Indians however still displaying a great deal of mistrust.[4]

This agreement allowed the French freedom ashore for a stay
that would last some two weeks. The Tahitians bartered fairly for
the foodstuffs and other supplies Bougainville needed, and were
evidently keenly aware of the value and usefulness of European
tools, displaying a light-fingered expertise at thievery when barter
did not work. The Tahitians shrewdly perceived the French needs,
and provided for them to obtain the things they wanted from the
two marvellous sailing emporiums. The interest in sex displayed by

the mostly young men of both ships' crews led to a profitable trade in nails and other useful items with the unmarried young women of the lower social class of the Tahitians, who, it soon turned out, viewed unrestricted and enthusiastic sexual activity as a sort of delicious hobby to be enjoyed before the responsibilities of marriage intervened. This sexual access was by no means universal: married women maintained a formal chastity similar to European women, and in the social rankings, women of the island's nobility were far more selective in the granting of their favours than the commoners, albeit with a refreshing candour and none of the priggishness and deceit that arguably characterized European dalliances. The freedom and naturalness with which the Tahitians embraced sexuality enchanted the French, although they were astonished to find that public sexual intercourse was accepted, and even offered as a kind of social hospitality. Bougainville marvelled:

> During the stay, several Frenchmen had cause to praise the country's customs. As they went into houses, they were presented with young girls, greenery was placed on the ground, and with a large number of Indians, men and women making a circle around them, hospitality was celebrated, while one of the assistants was singing a hymn to happiness accompanied by the sounds of a flute.[5]

For Bougainville, unaware of the total character of the society amidst which he had landed, a dismayed veteran of the savagery of the Seven Years' War which had challenged so deeply his *philosophe* optimism, and steeped in a study of the classics and a vanished, Arcadian golden age, the leap of assumption about the white-robed, handsome Tahitians was too much to resist. He wrote in his journal:

> Our white skin delights them, they express their admiration in this regard in the most expressive manner. Furthermore, the race is superb, with men 5 feet 10 inches tall, many reaching six feet, a few

exceeding this. Their features are very handsome.
They have a fine head of hair they wear in various
ways. Several also have a long beard which they rub
as they do their hair with cocoanut oil [*monoi*]. The
women are pretty and, something that is due to the
climate, their food and the water, men and women
and even old men have the finest teeth in the world.
These people breathe only rest and sensual pleasures.
Venus is the god they worship. The mildness of the
climate, the beauty of the scenery, the fertility of the
soil everywhere watered by rivers and cascades, the
pure air unspoiled by even those legions of insects
that are the curse of hot countries, everything
inspires sensual pleasure. And so I have named it
New Cythera [birthplace of Aphrodite], and the
protection of Minerva is as necessary here as in the
ancient Cythera to defend oneself against the influence of both the climate and the people's morals.[6]

Bougainville would carry this idealized vision back with him to
France after the short stay in Tahiti, although he had arguably
been shown only what the Tahitians wanted him to see. On his
arrival back in France he sensed that there would be public interest in his explorations amongst a population still smarting from
the defeats of the Seven Years' War, hungry for accomplishment,
and heavily influenced, as all were, in the exciting new spirit of
exploration that the war's end had released. Even without the scientific observations of his scholars left behind on Île de France, he
rushed into print a slim pamphlet entitled *An Account of M. de
Bougainville's Recent Discovery of an Island which He Has Named
New Cythera*. In it, he expanded on some of the observations from
his journal and added postscriptive commentary and discussion,
on the theme of the discovery of a proven example of a nobler,
simpler, more fulfilling human culture. It went off in French —
and European — intellectual society, and later in the reading public, like a mortar shell. He followed it with a more thorough and

rewritten account of the voyage in 1771, entitled simply *A Voyage Round the World*, which appeared in English translation in 1772.

Bougainville's writings, joined to a lurid interpretation of James Cook's views on Tahiti written by Dr. John Hawkesworth in Britain, cemented in the European mind a powerful if inaccurate vision of Paradise Found, a confirmation of much of what Rousseau and thinkers of his ilk had been arguing. It would have enormous impact on the ferment of discontent that led eventually to the great revolutionary upheaval at the end of the century, for here, it seemed, a classless social order based on simplicity, love and its joys, and a general bounty — available to all, not just an elite — truly existed.

Bougainville's little *Account* was not altogether an unblemished view of Tahitian society as he saw it — there is mention of human sacrifice and a few other dark shadows — but by and large it portrayed a culture of idyllic bliss:

> The climate of this island is mild and temperate, the air pure and serene, and the sky there is lovely.... The race is handsome. The women particularly are distinguished by the regularity of their features, their gentleness, and their natural affability. These women are free of any base interest.... The islanders live in peace among themselves, and know neither hatred, quarrels, dissension, nor civil war; they have no offensive or defensive weapons... The New Cytherans do not know anything of the major crimes: they abhor them as do all well-policed and wise nations.[7]

This sort of glowing praise would be echoed by Commerson, who, on his return from the Indian Ocean, wrote of his own admiration for the Tahitians in equally heartfelt terms:

> Then [consider] the simplicity of their moral code:
> the fairness of their treatment of women, who are

in no way oppressed, as is the case with most savages; their brotherly love to each other; their horror at the shedding of man's blood; their deep ven-
eration for the dead, who are supposed to be only
sleeping; their hospitality to strangers.... The
Tahitian has no property of his own; he offers and
generously presents anything as soon as he sees that
someone wishes for it, and therefore has never recognized any exclusive proprietary right.[8]

There was not only the unnerving message in these writings
that a simpler and better life, rather than the complex and painful
existence of most Europeans, was possible and now proven, but
that some of the most sacred underpinnings of the vastly unfair
Western social fabric — such as the right of private property —
were being challenged. To some receiving this message, it was
intellectual sedition of the most disturbing form toward the
ordered, layered, privilege-based world of the eighteenth century.
As Alan Moorehead observes:

If Tahiti was so perfect a place as they claimed it
was, then the idea of progress was nonsense: and
this was intolerable. Unregenerate luxury of the
South Sea kind was immoral and had to be
denounced — otherwise, how was one going to
endure the hard humdrum life of the West?[9]

Jean-Jacques Rousseau's essay on how inequality came to exist
in human society was written in 1754, and thus his arguments
were still fresh in the general mind when Bougainville's reports
seemed to provide their proof. The European social order of the
day was stratified, complex and stiflingly rigid, based on systemic
inequality that limited any chance of happiness, in practical terms,
to a tiny fraction of the population. There were as yet no constructive solutions being offered to this grinding unfairness and
drudgery, problems that, ironically, consumed the elite in their

salon discussions more than it did the struggling, apathetic mass of humanity whose labour supported them. The reports of warrior savagery in the horrors of the Seven Years' War had dashed hopes that the Noble Savage could be found in North America, at least insofar as Europeans conceived of nobility. But the vast, untouched Pacific could surely be home to a purer, less polluted society. At the moment of intellectual need for the confirmation of such a culture's existence, Bougainville, and Cook after him, seemed to have provided it. As Dunmore observes:

> Bougainville's elegant prose, buoyed by classical allusions, Commerson's enthusiastic reports to friends at home, comments by [the Prince of Nassau] and a number of the younger officers, helped to create the legend of Tahiti, a South Sea island paradise where the backbreaking labour of the peasants back home was unnecessary, where the sun shone over sparkling sands, and where men and women were free from the complex and irksome restrictions morality and property-owning imposed on sexual relations. The legend did not survive in this form for very long, but enough of it was left, even after the end of the Romantic era, for the very name of Tahiti ... to retain its aura of magic and idleness.[10]

The bloom of Bougainville's vision of a classical Arcadia began to fade with the publication of James Cook's second and third voyage volumes, written in what some perceived as a far more objective clarity than the lurid imaginings of Hawesworth, the ghostwriter of Cook's first account. Other navigators were visiting Tahiti and were writing of the people in a more plausible, if less idealized, light. Among them was the British astronomer William Wales, whose own experience of Tahiti was less than idyllic — he thought the women were too squat and heavy, to begin with — and who drily reflected about Bougainville's account:

The face of the country [Tahiti], making some allowance for a warm imagination, is not badly described by Mr. Bougainville; but some allowances must be made by every person, who has not seen the place, and would not be deceived. That gentleman seems to have been almost lost in admiration of its beauties, and those of its inhabitants all the time he was here. His colouring is indeed so high, that one cannot help suspecting a false glance; for his description suits much better with Mahomet's Paradise, than any terrestrial region.[11]

Wales, it should be noted, had seen Tahiti after its people and culture had begun to succumb to the impact of the European arrival; and the reality of Tahitian society when Bougainville found it held, in fact, much of what he claimed it did. The natural bounty of the island did offer the ability to make a living with little effort; the climate was gentle and supportive; physical beauty lay on every hand; and the Tahitians were handsome men and women given to warmth and kindness in their personal nature. The sexual availability of the adventurous single women was a matter of record, and certainly no sinfulness was linked with sexuality, as it was in European thought.

To a degree, however, Bougainville saw what the Tahitians wished him to see, and had arrived at a moment when the darker side of Tahitian society was not on display, although he was aware of human sacrifice. Tahiti, in contrast to the image of a classless, egalitarian society, was in fact a rigidly hierarchical community with strict divisions between the classes and a power over life and death invested in the hands of the ruling stratum, the *ali'i*. Warfare, which existed, was fought between islands or communities with a pitiless ferocity that spared no one, and a vast and complex system of exclusions and limitations to behaviour — based on religion and chiefly prerogatives and called *tapu* — could bring instant death to a transgressor. A travelling society of entertainers, known as the *arioi*, wandered between communities and islands

presenting pageantry and drama characterized by an explicit eroti-
cism and public sexual performance that shocked Europeans,
including James Cook, who later viewed them. The *arioi* were
released from the obligations of parenthood and marriage, and the
children that resulted from their unfettered coupling were murdered at birth. The religious pantheon of the Tahitians — ironically as crowded as the Grecian — was a complex one of gods with
interlocking and conflicting powers and influence, the worship of
whom — or transgression against — could lead again to sudden
death or ritualized sacrifice if the complex *tapu* system was not
scrupulously observed. Eden was not without its serpents.

Europeans at first grasped at Bougainville's incomplete, and possibly wishful, view of Tahiti as a confirmation of theories they were
debating at that very moment. Diderot, a *philosophe*, friend of
Rousseau, and producer of the *Encyclopédie*, hailed it as such. But
then, as the eighteenth century progressed, a curious reaction
against the "soft primitivism" of the idyllic Tahitian image began to
develop, even as clearer eyes began to see the Tahitians in merely
human terms rather than the classical. In England in particular, a
prurient fascination with a life of indolent sexuality and ease became
not the goal of utopian social thinking, but a point of departure in
another direction. The Tahiti of legend and its supposed life would
lead only to a life of sloth, luxury and degeneration, anathema to
thinkers subconsciously conditioned by the astringent rigours of
Judeo-Christian self-denial. To achieve a true social revolution and
the liberation of mankind would require a so-called "hard primitivism" based on reassuringly European concepts of self-discipline,
courage, acceptance of pain and the capacity for endurance.[12]

The pursuit of humanity's utopia, then, would come in a
European model; Tahiti would be relegated to a goal for the slothful
or degenerate and become a place deemed to require conversion to
European rigour. But the concept of a free, gentle society in which
all could aspire to some degree of fulfillment and happiness had
nonetheless travelled back to Europe in Bougainville's ships, and
remained to influence the coming French Revolution and the
upheavals elsewhere on the continent during the early nineteenth

century. And in Britain, in 1797, it would find its way, oddly, into the unrest that very nearly brought down Britain's social order and which would take its most threatening form in the mass mutiny of the crews of the Royal Navy, in the messdecks and wardrooms of which were many men who had experienced Tahiti and in one way or another were victim to its gentle subversion.

The question of why Bougainville saw what he did in Tahiti, and wrote of it as he did, might simply be replied to by a factor of time limitation. Two weeks in an utterly alien society is not enough to accurately observe its true nature. Yet Bougainville was no stranger to native societies. He had fought alongside, and lived with, warriors of the Huron, the Iroquois and the western tribes, and had married a Shawnee and been adopted into a tribal clan. His classical training, his resilient optimism and his espousal of the Rousseauian ideas of human dignity within simplicity, coupled with a drive to find a distant, utopian society that may have lain within him ever since he read Charles de Brosses's musings on a mystical southern continent, all prepared him to believe the best about any native society if it offered even a glimpse of the Noble Savage and promised to banish his dismay at the horrors of warrior-style combat in North America. The ghastliness of the Iroquois torture stake, the misery of the South American Indian peasantry, the grubbing minimalism of the Guarani or the Pecherais had only increased, it seemed, in the romantic Bougainville the need to find a wholly admirable native society, if only to prove to his somewhat shaken optimism that such optimism was valid. So many of his hopes and aspirations had ended in taints of failure or defeat at the hands of politicians of immensely greater cynicism. If he saw in the Tahitians what he wished to see, and needed to see, he can perhaps be forgiven for it.

Chapter Eight

Revolutions: Glory and Danger in America and France

On his return to France, Bougainville found himself warmly welcomed by a court and a populace hungry for reasons to feel proud, even if the expedition had arguably achieved none of the major goals it had been assigned. A practical sea route to China had not been explored, a great southern continent had not been discovered, and even a side request that Bougainville collect spices in the Dutch East Indies to replant at Île de France was not met. The scientific tasks of the voyage were the most successful, and even these had yielded mixed results. As Kimbrough observes:

> Only one of the two principal scientific goals established for the voyage was carried out. [Bougainville] did correct the charts of the waters where he sailed, pinpointing accurately the islands themselves ... and other navigational hazards, a contribution which would benefit all sailing in these areas. The chance to discover and classify new forms of plant and animal life was not carried to its conclusion since Philibert Commerson never got around to writing up his findings before he died, although he had apparently found thousands of new specimens. In all, the foray into the unknown, although nobly conceived, was ... a general failure.[1]

Bougainville had brought back with him a Tahitian, Aotouru, an energetic and agreeable man of limited abilities — he could never quite master French — who adapted remarkably well to his life in Paris and accompanied Bougainville as he once again made the necessary social calls and visits to those who had befriended or helped him. The list had diminished: his *chère maman*, to his lasting sorrow, was gone, as were other backers. Madame de Pompadour had been replaced in the king's bedroom by the coarse and disinterested Comtesse du Barry. But he was welcomed back into the salon of the Helvétius family, and by old comrades such as the Chevalier de Lévis, now a duke, as well as the guides and teachers of his early life, including the mathematician d'Alembert and the astronomer Lalande. To the writer who early had inspired him, Charles de Brosses, and to the royal geographer, Robert de Vaugondy, Bougainville imparted his knowledge of the scope and size of the Pacific Ocean, and, in particular, what it did *not* contain.

In intellectual and philosophical circles, however, Bougainville came to face an increasingly cool reception, perhaps in part because of an apparent failure in the scientific purposes. There was also the surprising cooling of Rousseau, whose cosmology — which, one would have thought, Bougainville's glowing first accounts of Tahiti confirmed, and which popular imagination thought it did — did not provide for a simpler, nobler people who were at the same time shockingly promiscuous and excellent petty thieves. To Rousseau, social simplicity and nobility were necessary bedmates, but Bougainville was revealing very little nobility of the European sort: rather, a warm and animal humanity. It had to be the fault of Bougainville's ineptitude as an observer, Rousseau concluded:

> ... there are mainly four kinds of men who make long-term voyages: sailors, merchants, soldiers and missionaries. One can hardly expect the first three groups to furnish good observers....[2]

Bougainville's reply, in the introduction of his completed *A Voyage Round the World*, published in 1771, would be cutting:

> I am a voyager and a mariner, that is, a liar and an imbecile in the eyes of that group of lazy and haughty writers who, in the shade of their study, philosophize endlessly about the world and its inhabitants, and majestically subjugate nature to their imagination.[3]

The earthy realities of Tahitian life, hailed by the passionate and humane Bougainville, would ironically leave Bougainville at an arm's length of disdain from Rousseau and his colleagues even as, at first, the grand confirmation of the value of simple, austere societies had been made. The answer the disoriented Rousseauians triumphantly created for their own reassurance was, instead, the celebration of "hard primitivism": military valour, simple republican piety and virtue, hard work and plain bread. It would be Sparta, not Athens, that would lead to human happiness, but at the end of Rousseau's road would be found Napoleon and his bayonets, not the arms of the flower-laden girls of Tahiti.

Bougainville found himself treated with derision by the *Académie des Sciences*, and the *rouge* naval officers who constituted the majority membership of the *Académie de Marine* displayed, by ignoring him altogether, their equal scorn for Bougainville's middle-class origins and his "intrusion" into their naval fraternity. The attention he received at court, and the public applause for his circumnavigation, merely increased their resentment. When Bougainville's formal account of the voyage finally appeared in print, it sold modestly well, and its contents became the topic of much discussion in the salons, if not, except in terms of disparagement, in the ranks of *les rouges*.

As Bougainville completed his manuscript, the question of what to do with his bemused Tahitian companion, Aotouru, presented itself. Public sentiment was declaring that he should somehow be sent home to his Paradise, and the increasing strain his upkeep put upon Bougainville's modest bank account required a solution. Bougainville had funded much of the world voyage from the settlement the Spanish had given him in the Malouines transfer, and the cash-strapped navy was slow to repay bills he had placed before them. In 1770, Bougainville suggested to the navy that it arrange to ship Aotouru home and deduct the costs from what they owed him. Understandably, the navy agreed, and the Tahitian began a long journey homeward via the Indian Ocean colony at Île de France. Aboard a ship sent from there to gather spices in the East Indies — and take him home — Aotouru contracted smallpox and died, to be buried at sea.[4]

Bougainville now faced the decision of what next to do with his life. His personal assets were greatly depleted, and he needed employment. There was the book to finish, but that offered little chance for material success. The navy was pressing him to decide whether he would revert to his army colonelcy or stay with the navy. The negative aspects of the latter path were not inconsiderable: his rank as *capitaine de vaisseau* was lower than that he had obtained in the army; he was regarded as an *intru* by the powerful fraternity of *rouge* officers; and, even with his world voyage, he had little experience of formal naval operations, fleet and squadron tactics, and sea warfare in general. Nonetheless, he chose to remain with the navy, and on January 31, 1770, he received his permanent commission as *capitaine de vaisseau*, attached to the Brest fleet, where he was expected to take up his duties as soon as he had secured publication of *A Voyage Round the World*.[5]

Even as he was completing the book, Bougainville had been planning another possible expedition, of a very different nature than a circumnavigation in tropical seas. In a discussion with Jean-Dominique Cassini, the assistant astronomer at the *Académie des Sciences*, Bougainville developed a plan for a comprehensive voyage of scientific investigation in search of both a potential Northwest Passage across North America to the Pacific, and the location of the North Pole itself, in ice-strengthened ships. A detailed concept was drawn up and presented to the king and the new minister of marine, Bourgeois de Boynes, whose responses were awaited. In the meantime, to provide Bougainville with income to supplement his meagre naval pay, his uncle, Jean Potentin d'Arboulin, suggested to Louis XV that Bougainville could well perform the occasional duties of *secrétaire de la chambre et du cabinet du roi*. The king agreed, and while Bougainville awaited the reply to his polar voyage concept, he took up his secretarial duties on April 18, 1772. The decision of de Boynes, a *rouge*, about the polar trip was soon forthcoming, and it was in the form of a curt refusal that rudely suggested that Bougainville had proposed it merely to line his own pockets. Stung, the new secretary to Louis XV replied, "Do you imagine, Monsieur, that I should have an easy time of it, high pay, and hardly any work to do?"[6]

De Boynes, who was ruthlessly ramming through some naval reforms, was adamant. There would be no polar expedition, and as soon as His Most Christian Majesty could spare him, the navy wished Bougainville to get on with learning the work of a professional naval officer — would *capitaine de vaisseau* Bougainville please oblige the navy, at his earliest convenience? Meanwhile, the growing hostility amongst *philosophes* to the unsettling image Bougainville had painted of the Tahitians had found resolution in Diderot's pamphlet *A Supplement to the Voyage of Bougainville*, which appeared in 1772 and made the rounds of the excited salons. It declared that Bougainville and his men, as proxies for all Europe, had polluted the Tahitians: the noble simplicity of the islanders *had* existed, and had been perverted by the intrusion of *La Boudeuse* and *Étoile*, undermining their happiness forever. There was a grain of truth in what Diderot said, but Bougainville was in no mood to reflect on it objectively. With de Boynes' caustic orders ringing in his ears, and a new identity in Parisian intellectual society as the Defiler of Eden, Bougainville went morosely off to Brest to devote himself to his naval career.[7]

When he arrived in Brest, Bougainville found that he would only be required to actually serve at sea for a quarter of the time; the bulk of his time would be devoted to duties ashore, to which he was allowed to include, as needed, his tasks as secretary to the king. Grudgingly, he was admitted to the *Académie de Marine*, but the *rouge* officers limited him to adjunct membership, obstensibly because of his duties at court. He soon found, however, that he was *not* to be employed at sea — he begged for any ship, to be sent on any purpose, but was refused. He would spend until April 1774 in a frustrating cycle of largely idle service in Brest, where he was shunned by the *rouge* elite; followed by attendance to the king, which was largely symbolic; a brief descent into the social whirl of Paris; and then back to the austerity and exclusion of Brest. His plight was scarcely changed by the death, in that month, of Louis XV. The new king, Louis XVI, retained Bougainville in his post, but the departure soon after of de Boynes from the naval ministry gradually produced some more employment for Bougainville at Brest. Characteristically, he had consoled himself with immersion in the treatises of naval tactics, signalling, gunnery, fleet and squadron manoeuvres and other naval arts, and from 1775 to 1777 he found himself called to serve — at sea — on the staff of several experienced admirals (among them de Guichen, de Chaffault and de la Motte Picquet) who valued this encyclopedic new knowledge. Command of a front-line warship was still denied to him, however.

Luck now entered the equation when he became a warm friend of a young *rouge* officer, the Duc de Chartres, who had entered the navy late and whom Bougainville guided and instructed. De Chartres was named as *chef d'escadre* (commodore) of a squadron more for his noble rank than any experience, and he had Bougainville appointed as *seconde* of his flagship, *La Solitaire*. This position, equivalent to the executive officer of a modern warship, provided Bougainville with a demanding introduction to day-to-day responsibility for the ship and its "people." He seems to have passed this rigorous test with good marks, and by retaining de Chartres's friendship and blunting other *rouge* hostility by being above criticism in his execution of his duties, he found himself in midsummer 1777 appointed to command the *Bien Aime*, a powerful seventy-four-gun vessel able to lie in the "line of battle" — not a minor warship. With this appointment,

Bougainville's tardy apprenticeship in his newly minted naval career was complete.[8]

Across the Atlantic, Great Britain's rebellious American colonies were into their second year of proclaimed independence, and were fighting a largely losing battle — so far — against the British armies sent to prevent them from throwing off the colonial yoke. But then, in 1777, the rebels defeated a large British force, marching south from Canada along Bougainville's Lake Champlain route under Lieutenant General John Burgoyne, who had intended to split New England from the other colonies by linking with British forces at New York. The news of the American victory at Saratoga, New York, convinced France that the colonists might conceivably win. French enthusiasm for the American cause had also been increased by the rustic charm of Benjamin Franklin, who had been sent to Paris to try to lure that country into an alliance. Franklin's studied "noble simplicity" — no dissolute Tahitian sybarite here, but a homespun son of the soil — and negotiating skills led to a declaration by a sympathetic France on December 17, 1777, that it would recognize the independence of the American colonies and conclude a treaty of alliance. This pact, confirmed on February 6, 1778, was followed by an astonishing burst of vengeful diplomacy by the French, which secured Holland and Spain as active allies against Britain, while much of the rest of Europe declared itself neutral. Having effectively isolated the British, France now looked to provide the actual support the Americans would need to win the war. The long-awaited revenge for the humiliations of the Seven Years' War was at hand. There would be arms, and troops, but the navy would provide the vital tool; and much to the good fortune of France it had been rebuilt and reorganized by the reforms of de Boynes and his successors into a far more capable force than the one so utterly defeated by Britain's Royal Navy in 1759 and 1760.

Early in 1778, the new minister of marine, the Comte de Sartine, assembled a squadron of warships at Toulon in the Mediterranean for service in North American waters. Its orders would be to provide assistance to the American colonists and use

Britain's distracted state to recapture the islands of the West Indies lost during the previous war. In command, with a rank equivalent to vice admiral, would be the Comte d'Estaing. Bougainville, alongside at Brest, received orders on March 15 to repair to Toulon, where he would take command of *Le Guerrier*, armed with seventy-four guns, which had been built in 1751 and was therefore quite elderly compared to the other vessels in the squadron. When he arrived in Toulon on March 30, Bougainville found he would be commanding an undermanned and badly equipped vessel in poor repair, crewed predominantly by conscript Provençal seamen who spoke no French, and that the squadron would depart on a transatlantic voyage to a theatre of war in two weeks. He wrote, in some exasperation:

> I had to create a personal staff like I already had at Brest, scare up cabin boys and the food for the damned captain's mess, all this in one week in a region where I didn't know a soul.... I don't even know Provencal, and I often have to have an interpreter in order to carry out my various tasks.[9]

When the squadron finally sailed from Toulon's *grande rade* on April 13, it had grown to twelve ships of the line, including *Le Guerrier*, fourteen frigates and thirty-six transports laden with seasick troops. Bougainville had managed, through a superhuman effort, to complete the acquisition and loading of necessary supplies and render the ships' rig operable, but there had been no time for training, many men had deserted before sailing, and, during the tortuous fifty-two-day passage to North America, made longer by preparatory manoeuvres d'Estaing had ordered in the Mediterranean, the strain on Bougainville became enormous. He wrote in his journal:

> Since our departure I have been tired out, being on deck day and night without other help than that of the boatswain who, excellent fellow though he is, has, like myself, been half killed with work.[10]

Of Bougainville's complement of officers, nothing is revealed; it was a long way from the efficient and close-knit wardroom of *La Boudeuse* in the faraway Pacific.

D'Estaing's leisurely crossing of the Atlantic, combined with problems coordinating with the leadership of the rebellious colonists, meant that the French missed an opportunity to attack the principal British squadron under Howe, which was at anchor in New York Harbor. D'Estaing withdrew instead to Newport, Rhode Island, to support an American attack on that port. He learned abruptly that Howe had industriously got himself to sea and followed the French, and now had them trapped. By dint of surprisingly good seamanship, d'Estaing managed to slip out to sea past Howe's blockade, and now it was Howe's turn to steer for New York with the larger French force in pursuit. A storm prevented a conclusive engagement, and rather than resume hovering off Newport — which the Americans had not yet captured — d'Estaing opted to take his squadron into Boston for rest and repairs at the end of August.

The French had been at sea for four months, and the conditions in the ships were appalling. Bougainville had raged over d'Estaing's real or perceived reluctance to take some decisive action, in large part because of the deteriorating state of his crew. He wrote:

> In God's name, let us decide and then act, and when once we have secured the safety of the squadron, then men will at least enjoy the rest they have deserved. I observe, with profound sorrow, that it is always usual at councils and discussions to pay no heed whatsoever to the physical condition of our soldiers and sailors, as if their health was not the basis of all operations.[11]

This humanitarian concern for his crew's welfare marked Bougainville throughout his career. The men, and their families, remembered, his sympathy for the plight of common men stood him in good stead during the turbulent days of the revolution.

There had been a few moments of pathos; at one point, the young Marquis de la Fayette, in American service, had come aboard *Le Guerrier* and presented an astonished Bougainville with Montcalm's sword, which he carried on his last day on the Plains of Abraham. Bougainville was touched:

> With tears in my eyes I kissed it, and it became even more precious to me for the sake of the young and valiant *chevalier* at whose hands I received it.[12]

In Boston — thankfully free of attack from the British, who were hesitant to engage so strong a force — relations with the Americans were difficult and exasperating, for it was not that long since the days when the French threat to the north engendered a mortal enmity in the *bostonnais*. Bougainville was asked to oversee the construction of some defensive works ashore, and complained that "fifty Americans have not done in three weeks what thirty of our soldiers have completed in one. You cannot imagine how slow and lazy the people of this country are." He wandered the town in off-duty hours, but friction between the French and Bostonians led to fighting in the streets and several deaths. Amidst this tension, Bougainville was reminded again of his previous service, and life, in North America. As Kimbrough relates:

> A small delegation of Iroquois appeared in the city. One of them was the grandson of Chief Onoraguete, who had adopted Bougainville into the clan of the turtle. The young Indian was, so to speak, Bougainville's nephew, for his mother was sister to [Ceuta,] the Indian woman Bougainville was given as his wife, daughter of Onoraguete.[13]

Bougainville greeted his nephew and the other warriors with warmth and hospitality, but the *rouge* officers added this, which they considered an undesirable relationship, to the growing list of resentments they held against him. The day when the *rouges* would have their moment to strike at the *intru* was not far off.

In November, d'Estaing sailed from Boston and its inhospitable population — "The American women, virtuous or otherwise, have no liking for the French; so you can guess how fond we are of them," sighed Bougainville — arriving in Martinique in early December. There, an attempt would be made to recapture former French possessions in the Caribbean. A first attempt to retake St. Lucia failed, with *Le Guerrier* suffering a few casualties from shore fire, but St. Vincent was taken, as was Grenada, off which a confused, ill-led and inconclusive sea battle was fought — *La Guerrier* lay in the middle of the French line with no significant role.

By the coming of 1779, the French had largely been successful in the Caribbean program of recaptures, but now a new challenge arose. The British were campaigning successfully through Georgia on the mainland, and had made Savannah their base of operations. D'Estaing sailed north to assist the rebel resistance by using his squadron and troops to lay siege to Savannah. It took the summer to prepare for the expedition, but finally it sailed, arriving at Savannah on September 1, 1779. The troops were landed and the siege undertaken for six frustrating weeks: to no avail. By early November, the demoralized troops were re-embarked and d'Estaing sailed for France, having achieved some success in the Caribbean but none at all in support of the American land war or in defeating the Royal Navy squadron. And the cost in men and equipment, particularly in the fever-ridden Caribbean, had been appalling. Bougainville had poured out his frustrations into his journal as the Savannah siege dragged on and fever coursed through both the encampments ashore and the gundecks afloat:

> Still another announce protraction of the campaign; but will the ships withstand the extension; will the men? They get worse every day … at least 40 [in *La Guerrier*] are condemned to death…. The ambitious [d'Estaing] is aware of the conditions of the ships and the men, and he doesn't seem to care in the least. Of all the accursed plagues on mankind, an ambitious master is the worst…. Never has there been a more

crying abuse of excessive authority; never has excessive authority been put in worse hands.[14]

In truth, if d'Estaing had been timid about grappling with the
British — a charge not entirely defensible — he had manoeuvred
the French squadron at least as well as the British had handled
theirs. The *marine royale* of France of these few years was almost on
a par with the Royal Navy of Britain in coping with the vagaries
and limitations of eighteenth-century ship technology, weather,
disease and luck. Where Bougainville's great rage was directed was
toward the suffering of his men; it had not been through indifference that *La Boudeuse's* crew had survived the circumnavigation so
well. In this, as James Cook had proved in the Royal Navy,
Bougainville was ahead of the times in simple concern and responsibility for what happened to his people: he did not share
d'Estaing's apathy. The humanitarian heart still beat more strongly
in his chest than the warrior's.

Le Guerrier reached Rochefort on December 15, 1779, and an
exhausted Bougainville went wearily ashore to find that he had
been — despite his raging frustrations — promoted to the equivalent of rear admiral. The posting, however, was junior to that of a
rouge officer of far less experience. Seething, Bougainville politely
refused the appointment, seeing it as symptomatic of the wasteful
and unfair subordination of *bleu* officers to the *rouges*. The navy
accepted his letter without comment, and the king bestowed upon
him a retirement rank of major general in the army and a modest
pension. That date of appointment, January 28, 1780, appeared to
mark the end of his naval career.

Retiring first to Paris and then to his small estate,
Bougainville, who was now fifty, unexpectedly found romance in
his life in the person of a beautiful young woman two decades his
junior, who came of an excellent family. Her name was Flore-
Josèphe de Montendre, and their mutual attraction and affection
were immediate, heartfelt and lasting. Bougainville made the necessary application to marry, which was granted, to the king. The
wedding was to wait until the end of the year, however;

Bougainville had come ashore from *Le Guerrier* ill and exhausted, and his doctor had found an alarming scrotal tumour which had to be removed by surgery. Bougainville's recovery was successful, if lengthy, and Flore-Josèphe received a fully fit husband — in all respects — when the wedding finally occurred. She was, ironically, the daughter of a *rouge* naval captain, and she would prove a strong and devoted companion who understood the demands of naval life. The marriage would produce four children, and Bougainville's love for her, quite feelingly expressed ("You know, Mademoiselle, I love you with all the tenderness of which a heart is capable," he would write, while courting her) was reciprocated with warmth and passion. This solid union gave Bougainville much emotional strength, which would prove of great value in the tests that yet lay ahead.

Even as he had hardly begun his convalescence, however, his retirement from the navy was set aside, by order of the king. The various ministries were preparing to remount their efforts to support the American colonists, and Bougainville's creditable service under d'Estaing simply made him too valuable to leave ashore. On February 16, 1780, Bougainville received notice that his retirement had been rescinded, and he was recalled to service. In deference to his ongoing recovery and impending marriage, however, he was appointed to command of the eighty-gun *Languedoc*, which lay at Brest and would not sail throughout 1780. In the new year, as soon as Bougainville had reported that he was fit for service, he was ordered out of *Languedoc*, promoted to *chef d'escadre* (commodore), and sent to hoist his broad pendant in *L'Auguste*, a first-class fighting vessel armed with eighty guns, which also lay at Brest. A fleet was being assembled there, comprising three squadrons, of which Bougainville would command one. The fleet was to be commanded by Lieutenant General the Comte de Grasse, in the huge ninety-eight-gun *Ville de Paris*, and its first task would be to sail to Newport, Rhode Island, and absorb a small French squadron already there, under Barras. The fleet sailed from Brest in March 1781, making a competent, thirty-eight-day crossing to Martinique. During the crossing,

Bougainville instituted amongst the ships of his squadron a requirement for gunnery and seamanship training that soon brought it to a fair state of efficiency. Once at sea, he also established an excellent relationship with his flag captain in *L'Auguste*, de Castellan, who shared his views on the health of the crew and the need for cleanliness, training and discipline. By the time the French arrived in the Windward Islands, de Grasse had, in *L'Auguste* and much of the remainder of the fleet, a competence and efficiency rarely achieved in the French navy since the heady days of the 1690s.[15]

Once in the West Indies, de Grasse darted about the islands in a cat-and-mouse chase with a British squadron under Sir Samuel Hood that produced no decisive clash. The French took the small island of Tobago, but no action of serious consequence took place until July, when de Grasse escorted a merchant convoy to Haiti and found letters there from George Washington, commanding the American army, asking in the strongest terms if he would bring the French fleet, along with any Caribbean garrison troops that could be spared, to Chesapeake Bay, on the shores of which a climactic confrontation was building with the British army under Lord Cornwallis. Taking a circuitous route through the Bahamas, so as not to be intercepted by British cruisers, de Grasse had not yet arrived at the mouth of the Chesapeake when a British fleet under Graves arrived there, found no French ships, and sailed off again for New York. Behind them, by more luck and coincidence than planning, de Grasse arrived in the Chesapeake on August 30 and was joined by Barras, who had got away from Newport and had siege guns for the army embarked aboard. Ashore, the force confronting Cornwallis was a combined Franco-American one, commanded by Washington and, for France, Rochambau. They were uncoiling a plan to entrap and force the surrender of the British land forces in the southern colonies on the narrow peninsula that held the village of Yorktown, Virginia. With that surrender secured, the French navy could then move French and American troops anywhere in the southern colonies to defeat any remaining British activity. It was clear at once that this was a plan that could end the Revolutionary War: Britain would sue for peace. Bougainville, remembering the chaos and lost opportunities of the previous expedition under d'Estaing, was privately skeptical:

> We received news yesterday from Messrs. Washington and Rochambau. They have marched to the head of [Chesapeake] Bay … and they ask that we come get them there in order to join Messrs. La Fayette and Saint-Simon. If that juncture took place, Cornwallis' fate would be decided…. I certainly fear that no one will do what is necessary to execute this plan, just as useful as it is glorious.[16]

Cornwallis had carried out a campaign over two years to subdue the southern colonies, and had withdrawn to await reinforcement by sea before assaulting Virginia. The Americans and French had pursued him. The question now had become which naval force would secure command of the Chesapeake, for if the British did, Cornwallis would escape the trap Washington was setting and the war would carry on. But if France could hold those waters, even briefly enough to allow Cornwallis to be attacked from landward, British hopes for subjugation of the southern colonies would be at an end, and with them, any hope of winning the war.

Rear Admiral Thomas Graves' fleet, which had missed de Grasse's arrival at the Chesapeake, reversed course on arrival at New York when word was brought out to him that Barras had sailed from Newport for the Chesapeake. As Graves' nineteen men-o'-war sailed south, they had no idea that in Chesapeake Bay they would be met, not by Barras's small squadron, but by de Grasse's twenty-four line-of-battle ships, including Bougainville in *L'Auguste.*

The French had been riding at anchor awaiting news of the entrapment process that Washington and Rochambau were conducting against Cornwallis, who was in a defensive position at Yorktown with his back to the sea. On the morning of September 5, a patrolling frigate at sea off the main French anchorage reported an approaching naval force to the north, too large to be the expected Newport squadron. By virtue of a favourable ebb tide, de Grasse was able to get his fleet to sea. It was organized into its three fighting divisions: the leading element, the "van," or *avant-garde*, was commanded by Bougainville in his eighty-gun flagship, *L'Auguste*, and consisted of eight ships of sixty-four guns or more; the "centre," or *corps de bataille*, commanded by de Latouche-Tréville in the flagship *Ville de Paris* (ninety-eight guns) and consisting of eight ships equal in power to the van; and the "rear," or *arrière-garde*, commanded by de Monteil in the eighty-gun *Languedoc* and consisting of eight ships, most of them with seventy-four guns. Advancing on them from seaward was a British fleet of nineteen ships, the majority of them seventy-four-gunners, divided similarly into three divisions.

The uncertain wind conditions and the difficulty in manoeuvring the vessels meant that most of the day was taken up assembling the respective fleets into two long lines which gradually converged on one another. By shortly after 4 p.m., the lines were close enough for gunnery to begin, but as the British vessels closed on the French their contact was principally with the eight ships of Bougainville's van. From his command position on the open quarterdeck of *L'Auguste*, Bougainville conducted a dogged, toe-to-toe broadside battle with the British line in a storm of roiling smoke and thunder in which the French gunnery and determination inflicted astonishing damage on the British. This was not the French navy of 1759, and at last Bougainville had his major, decisive battle with his enemy. We can only speculate about his thoughts at finally coming to grips with the adversary before whom he had paused on the Plains of Abraham in that long-ago September. Now, in another September, he was again challenged by a face-to-face confrontation, and if there had been doubt of his fighting valour — to himself, as well as to others — the resolution and gritty courage he was to display in these two bloody and wreckage-strewn hours would put it to rest. *L'Auguste* fought at close gunnery range with British warships of its size and power, giving away nothing but inflicting much damage, until finally, with the coming of darkness, the action was broken off.

De Grasse had not routed the British — the entire fleets did not become fully engaged — but Bougainville had fought them to a draw. The Royal Navy steered away northward, leaving the sea to the French. Sir Samuel Hood, commanding the British van with which Bougainville had traded blow for blow and inflicted the heaviest damage sustained by British warships at the hands of an enemy in forty years, commented drily when Graves asked what should be done:

> If it was wished I should say more, it would be only that we should get into the Chesapeake to the suc-cour of Lord Cornwallis and his brave troops if possible, but that I was afraid the opportunity of doing it was passed by, as doubtless de Grasse had most effectively barred the entrance against us, which was what human prudence suggested we ought to have done against him.... Sir Samuel would be very glad to send an opinion, but he really knows not what to say in the truly lamentable state we have brought ourselves.[17]

De Grasse returned to anchor in the Chesapeake, in command of its waters, where he was now joined by Barras's squadron. Ashore, deprived of naval support, supplies or rescue, Cornwallis succumbed to a combined French and American frontal assault on his fortifications, and surrendered on October 17, 1781. Two days later, on October 19, at 2 p.m., Cornwallis's army marched out of Yorktown to lay down its arms, to the tune of a march entitled *The World Turned Upside Down*. As the American historian Joseph Mitchell succinctly summarizes:

> This surrender virtually ended the war in America, although some fighting continued on the Ohio fron-tier, in South Carolina and Georgia. The king was of a mind to continue the war, but the British people were overwhelmingly opposed. The ministry fell: a

new cabinet was appointed. General Sir Guy Carleton superseded [British commander] Clinton in the spring of 1782, and shortly after assuming the command in New York wrote Washington asking for a cessation of hostilities. The treaty of peace acknowledging the independence of the United States of America was formally ratified on September 3, 1783.[18]

Bougainville was ashore following the surrender, and in the presence of Washington, La Fayette and Rochambau, de Grasse turned to him and said simply, "the laurels of the engagement belong to you."[19]

The wheel of fate had turned full circle for Bougainville, and a debt of sorts had been repaid. On a fateful day in 1759 he had hesitated, and a continent might have been lost at that moment to the enemy. Now, in 1781, he did not waver, and the continent had arguably been won back from that enemy. These were laurels indeed — and, to a degree, laurels of redemption.

The war would not end on such a note of success for Bougainville, highlighting again the increasingly embittered struggle between *rouge* and *bleu* officers. De Grasse had returned with the French fleet to the West Indies for the winter, and had conducted confused and disappointing actions with varied success against the British, until a major fleet action against a British fleet under Rodney took place on April 12, 1782, off the small island group of *les Saintes*. Bougainville again commanded the van with his pendant flying in *L'Auguste*, but on this occasion, whether by design or accident, Rodney disregarded the protocol of engaging in two parallel lines and burst through the French line well back from the van. The unexpected and daring action took the French by surprise. *L'Auguste*'s rigging was heavily damaged by British broadsides from astern, and she drifted into inoperability.

Bougainville hoisted signals ordering his squadron to go about to the defence of the centre and rear, which were being severely mauled in the unexpected, confused clutch of ships banging away at point-blank range where the new British weapon, the short but murderous "carronade," was wreaking havoc. In the drifting clouds of gunsmoke, the signals were not seen, and on disengagement and the eventual return to France, Bougainville found himself subject to a court-martial brought against him by the *rouge* de Grasse, who claimed the defeat was the consequence of Bougainville's failure to double back and defend the centre of the French line against Rodney's attack. Behind de Grasse lay the *rouge* fraternity, with its long list of grievances against the *intru* Bougainville, of which the success off the Chesapeake was the most recent entry. When the final charges were drawn up, Bougainville found himself accused both of lack of seamanship ability and — a far more stinging charge — of cowardice under fire. It was an extraordinary allegation, given Bougainville's behaviour on the Chesapeake.

The court-martial hearing was finally convened in May of 1784, and after proceedings that included heated testimony from all officers involved in the action off *les Saintes*, the board of senior officers found the charges against Bougainville proven, but could not agree on a sentence; they settled for a public reprimand. Made the scapegoat for the loss, Bougainville appealed, but was turned down, then suffered the further humiliation of being banned from court by Louis XVI, who had been upset by the loss off *les Saintes*. It was a dark end to this chapter in Bougainville's life, and it came so soon after a moment of transcendent success. To Rodney would go the accolades of history, for his use of daring new tactics that foreshadowed those of Horatio Nelson and which were to prevent further losses to the French, notably in Jamaica. To Bougainville would go the lion's share of blame for the defeat. As Kimbrough observes of Rodney's victory:

> No British admiral had showed similar daring at the battle of Chesapeake Bay. There, where the outcome of the engagement was infinitely so much greater ... Bougainville's division had driven the enemy off. This momentous battle, on a much

smaller scale in regard to the number of ships shooting at each other, was largely forgotten in the wake of the more spectacular action at The Saints. That is one of the great ironies of history.[20]

Chapter Nine

A Life Well Lived

Bougainville returned from the American war shrouded in controversy and a degree of disgrace, to the enormous satisfaction of the *rouge* element in the navy. But if he now put off his uniform with a bitter taste in his mouth, he would soon be diverted by the sweetness of the home life he was now, unexpectedly, free to enjoy, since the navy was unlikely to employ him further. He and Flore-Josèphe added a modest Paris address to their properties, while remaining for the most part in domestic seclusion at La Brosse. Children now began to appear: four boys born in the course of the next five years, beginning with Hyacinthe in 1783. It became for Bougainville a rich and full life of near-retirement, and he displayed no lasting vitriol in his writings about the injustice of his reprimand and banishment. In another of the many ironies of his life, it was now that the *Académie de Marine* advanced him to full membership, in part because, as an inactive officer, he would be not be away at sea, and in part because the academy members may have perceived that Bougainville deserved better. It would not be until de Grasse's death on January 11, 1788, that Bougainville would find naval — and royal — favour slowly returning to him. For his part, de Grasse maintained to the end his denunciation of Bougainville for a failure that was, in retrospect, more a result of innovative British tactics, weaponry and the limitations of eighteenth-century shiphandling and signalling.

The great first test of his return to public life came in January of 1789, when he submitted an application for membership in the *Académie des Sciences*, which had ignored his circumnavigation, and membership in which was the greatest recognition to which a scientist or academic of any stripe could aspire. Louis XVI had to approve the candidates, and it seemed that all was forgiven, for the application was warmly accepted with uncommon alacrity. A few months later, in July of 1789, the simmering discontent within French society broke out into open unrest, and the Bastille in Paris was stormed and taken. Bougainville and Flore-Josèphe had been living simply at La Brosse — his modest naval pay allowed little more — and she had shared his sympathy and kindness toward citizenry of all classes. The anger directed toward the great hereditary nobility thus did not see Bougainville as a target. He was invited to attend a mass rally held in Paris in June of 1790 to celebrate the first anniversary of the fall of the Bastille, and an increasingly desperate naval ministry, aware of the high respect the common seamen had for Bougainville, astonished him with an offer of restitution to full service, promotion to the land rank of lieutenant general — de Grasse's rank — and command of all naval forces, ashore and afloat, at Brest.

It was an appointment that spoke well of Bougainville's humanitarian instincts, and the reputation he had earned for caring for the men he commanded, but Bougainville found, soon after he arrived in Brest on November 30, 1790, and hoisted his flag in *Majestueux*, that he was dealing with a social upheaval of far greater severity. The first threat to his authority came in a mutinous assembly in the line-of-battle ship *America*. Bougainville arrested seventeen ringleaders, but saw to it that they were treated leniently. Order seemed restored for a time: the former *bleu* officer with the warm human touch was perhaps what was necessary to keep the lid on the boiling social ferment within the navy. Bougainville tried to swim with the tide: he created a ceremony he hoped would bind the officers and seamen of his ships together in a greater sense of solidarity. It involved the raising of the new, *tricolore*-based naval ensign on all his ships, replacing the simple white Bourbon ensign, and Bougainville thrilled the men of the lower deck — and shocked the officers of more elevated social origins — by asking the petty officers and the gunner's mates to sit down with him at the celebratory meal.

But however high Bougainville was held in personal esteem, the larger anger and resentments of the seamen made the normal operation of a socially disciplined naval organization almost impossible, and Bougainville became exhausted from the effort, finally falling ill with an attack of dysentery. The family at home needed him, and he was wise enough to see that a considerate civility and the fine manners of a vanished era were of no value in his tumultuous command. On February 5, 1791, he tendered his resignation, hauling down his flag in *Majestueux*, and went home to Flore-Josèphe and the boys. He was sixty-one years of age.

The navy did not strike him from its list of officers, and in September of that year a harassed Louis XVI offered Bougainville the post of minister of marine when the Comte de Fleurier resigned in exasperation. Bougainville saw a thankless task in the offer, and declined it. Still, the navy would not let go: in January of 1792, the rank of vice admiral in a newly reorganized navy was offered to him. This time, Bougainville's reply was final and unequivocal:

> Duty and honour both forbid me to accept an eminent rank, the duties of which are beyond my powers.... Pray, Monsieur, be good enough to explain my feelings to the king, for I should be most unhappy were I unable to devote my declining days to the service of my country, and be able to end my career as I began it....[1]

The navy would seek him out no more, and it was a difficult decision, the navy pay being Bougainville's principal source of income. The family responded by consolidating: Bougainville sold the small estate at La Brosse — it was becoming vulnerable to wandering mobs — and bought a modest house near Anneville-sur-Mer on the Normandy coast. Here he installed Flore-Josèphe and the boys, then went to Paris to see what he could do to help ease the growing tumult. His gesture almost cost him his life, as he was in an audience with Louis XVI on June 20, when a mob burst into the Tuileries and forced the king to display himself to the crowds outside while wearing a revolutionary Phrygian stocking cap. The arrival of the Terror and the wholesale butchery that went on under the lunatic Robespierre prompted Bougainville to arrange for his family to leave the Normandy house and take refuge in St-Malo, where they were hidden in the cottage of a shipwright who had been part of the long-ago Malouines project. They were betrayed, however, and arrested; Bougainville was ordered taken to Paris, and execution by the guillotine was a virtual certainty when Robespierre fell and a degree of sanity returned. Bougainville gathered up a shaken Flore-Josèphe and the boys and withdrew again to Anneville, for what he thought would be a life of modest farming.

But France was not through with him. In 1795, "citizen Bougainville, farmer at Anneville," was appointed to the newly formed *École normale de Paris* by the revolutionary Directory, and this was followed by appointment to the *Bureau des longitudes* and the *Institut National* (*Institut de France*). He would present a number of papers at the latter institution, ranging from studies of North American natives to a bizarre proposal to bottle up Britain's Royal Navy in its ports by creating a line of buoys suspending huge chains to snag on British keels, off each port. The institute authorized a voyage to the South Seas to examine the coastline of Australia, and through Bougainville's efforts his son, Hyacinthe, went on the voyage. Bougainville sat on a committee that tested, and made positive recommendations to Napoleon on, a 1798 prototype of a submarine designed by Robert Fulton.

Bougainville's income began to improve because of this work, and the small house he had maintained at 56, rue de Bouloi for his Paris visits was proving impractical, as was the long migration back and forth from Anneville. In 1799, he and Flore-Josèphe bought a small chateau at Suisnes, about twelve miles north of Paris, which was intended to be their final home. The chateau was destined to be a place shrouded with sorrow, however, as in 1801, Amand de Bougainville, aged sixteen, drowned before his mother's eyes while swimming in the Yerres River beside the chateau. The experience shattered Flore-Josèphe, who declined in health thereafter without hope of recovery, and died on August 7, 1806. The three remaining boys would fare well: Hyacinthe returned from his Pacific voyage — having visited Tahiti — and would pursue a successful naval career, rising to rear admiral; Alphonse served with distinction in Napoleon's army, as did Adolphe, who rose to become a general in the cavalry.[2]

Bougainville's position in society was now secure. Napoleon appointed him to the senate in 1799, which increased his income from 4,000 francs to 25,000. After Napoleon declared himself emperor, he named Bougainville — whom he liked, and called "my dear royalist" — a Grand Officer in the Legion of Honour, and, three years later, a Count of the Empire. It was an extraordinary degree of recognition, possibly from a despot whose own remarkable intellect recognized and respected the scientific passion and common touch that Bougainville seems to have retained, even at this stage in his life.

By now a permanent resident of Paris — he had sold Suisnes, with its sad memories — Bougainville issued from his desk at the *Institut* a constant stream of papers and proposals, which were of varying value. Included in the list was a proposal that France enhance its imperial ambitions by colonizing the Malouines, which the Spanish had retitled the Malvinas but then largely abandoned. Napoleon, with his army mired in the Peninsular War against Wellington, gave the proposal little consideration. More characteristic of Bougainville's core nature was his effort to secure the release of the British naval explorer Matthew Flinders, who had been imprisoned on the island of Réunion, where he had put in after South Pacific explorations, unaware that war had broken out. Bougainville used his continuing membership in London's Royal Society to secure a pension for Flinders' destitute sister, and was instrumental in having Flinders himself freed from detention.

In 1809, the aged gentleman found himself faced with another of his life's many ironies when he was asked by the minister of marine to sit on a board of inquiry into the catastrophic naval defeat at Trafalgar in 1805 at the hands of the Royal Navy under Horatio Nelson. The charges were not directed at the French admiral in overall command, Villeneuve, but the *chef d'escadre* of the rear of the combined Franco-Spanish fleet, Dumanoir de Pelly. The allegations levelled against Dumanoir were essentially the same as Bougainville had faced after the battle off *les Saintes* a quarter-century earlier. Then, Bougainville had been convicted as much by the hatred of the *rouge* officers as by any facts. It gave enormous satisfaction to Bougainville to see Dumanoir tried fairly on the facts alone, and exonerated when he used a defence that had failed to win acquittal for Bougainville. It was a kind of bittersweet victory to grant Dumanoir's absolution, and another circle in Bougainville's life, similar to the one that linked the Plains of Abraham to the Chesapeake, had been closed.

Two years after this poignant exercise in vindication by proxy, Bougainville, now eighty-two, had a recurrent attack of dysentery. His sturdy form, which had withstood so many of the shocks of life, struggled for ten days, then surrendered. He died quietly on August 31, 1811, and Napoleon ordered that his remains be interred in the Pantheon — in a final irony, in the crypt that held Jean-Jacques Rousseau. Flore-Josèphe and Amand had been buried in the small cemetery of Saint-Pierre in Montmartre, and Napoleon ordered that Bougainville's heart be buried there with them. It was a gesture that spoke much of both men, regardless of the harsher judgments of history.

The achievements of Louis-Antoine de Bougainville's life were many, and he represented to a degree the ideal eighteenth-century gentleman, adept at arts and sciences and myriad other skills, executed effortlessly with grace and civility, even at the darkest moments. It was a model for civilized manhood soon to be swept away in a cataclysmic age of ruthless passions that had little need for the ways of literate, restrained men of refined abilities and a kind of universal citizenship. Yet, to his credit, Bougainville was recognized as bridging, in his own person, the gap between the cold rigidity of the vanished old order and the passionate excess of the new, because of his warmly humane instincts and the armour of his heart, worn on his sleeve throughout his life. It was this quality of warmth, of something born in a humanist spirit, that was Bougainville's greatest strength — in a rare moment of lucidity, Britain's George III had observed that Captain James Cook was a fine sailor, but Bougainville was an inspired one — and which brought him his greatest accolade, the unfeigned liking and respect of both the powerful and the common.[3]

In his determination to press forward through the disappointments and the adversities of his life, which never witnessed his decline into a meanness of spirit, there was also a model that invites study and emulation across the centuries. Richard Walter, who had served as surgeon in Lord Anson's flagship *Centurion* during its epic circumnavigation of 1740–44, observed of the struggles of that expedition:

> Though prudence, intrepidity and perseverance united are not exempted from the blows of adverse fortune, yet in a long series of transactions they usually rise superior to its power, and in the end rarely fail of proving successful.[4]

For the brave and compassionate heart of Louis-Antoine de Bougainville, buried with that of Flore-Josèphe, no more apt epitaph could be written.

Endnotes

CHAPTER ONE

1   David Ogg, *Europe of the Ancien Régime, 1715–1783* (New York: Harper & Row, 1965), 247.

2   Mary Kimbrough, *Louis-Antoine de Bougainville, 1729–1811: A Study in French Naval History and Politics* (Lewiston, N.Y.: Mellen Press, 1990), 3.

3   John Robson, "A Short Biography of Louis-Antoine de Bougainville," http://pages.quicksilver.net.nz/jcr/~boug2.html.

4   Kimbrough, *Bougainville*, 5.

5   Lincoln Davis Hammond, ed., *News from New Cythera: A Report of Bougainville's Voyage, 1766–1769* (Minneapolis, U. of Minnesota Press, 1970), 6.

6   Francis Parkman, *Montcalm and Wolfe* (1884; New York: Collier, 1962), 256.

CHAPTER TWO

1   Fred Anderson, *Crucible of War: The Seven Years' War and the Fate of Empire in British North America, 1754–1766* (New York: Knopf, 2000), *passim.*

2   Parkman, *Montcalm and Wolfe*, 255.

3   Ibid., 257.

4   Bougainville, to his brother Jean-Pierre, March 29, 1756, in Michael Ross, *Bougainville* (London: Gordon and Cremonesi, 1978), 21.

CHAPTER THREE

1   Bougainville, journal entry, July 2, 1756, in *Adventures in the Wilderness: The American Journals of Louis-Antoine de Bougainville, 1756–1760*, ed. Edward Pierce Hamilton (Norman, Okla.: University of Oklahoma Press, 1964), 4.

2   Anderson, *Crucible of War*, 151.

3   Ibid.

4   Bougainville, journal entry, July 11, 1756, in *Adventures in the Wilderness*, 9.

5   Bougainville, journal entry, July 29, 1756, ibid., 18.

6   D. Peter MacLeod, *The Canadian Iroquois and the Seven Years' War* (Toronto: Dundurn Press, 1996), 84.

7   Ibid., 79.

8   Ibid., 87.

9   Ibid., 88.

10 Bougainville, journal entry, August 9, 1756, in *Adventures in the Wilderness*, 24.

11 Bougainville, journal entry, August 10, 1756, ibid., 25.

12 Montcalm to minister, late 1756, cited in Étienne Taillemite, "Louis Antoine de Bougainville," in *Dictionary of Canadian Biography* (Toronto: U. of Toronto Press, n.d.), 5:103.

13 MacLeod, *The Canadian Iroquois*, 88.

14 Bougainville, journal entry, August 14, 1756, in *Adventures in the Wilderness*, 26.

15 Anderson, *Crucible of War*, 153.

16 Ross, *Bougainville*, 28.

17 Bougainville, journal entry, August 14, 1756, in *Adventures in the Wilderness*, 26.

18 Stephen Cross, journal entry, in Fred Anderson, *Crucible of War*, 154.

19 Ibid.

20 Bougainville, to Mme. Hérault, spring 1757, in Michael Ross, *Bougainville*, 39.

21 Bougainville, to his brother Jean-Pierre, spring 1757, ibid., 39.

22 Bougainville, to his brother Jean-Pierre, fall 1756, ibid., 33.

23 Kimbrough, *Louis-Antoine de Bougainville*, 9.

24 Bougainville, journal entry, January 8, 1757, in *Adventures in the Wilderness*, 78.

25 Bougainville, journal entries, May 12–15, 1757, ibid., 108.

26 Bougainville, journal entry, June 14, 1757, ibid., 115.

27 Bougainville, journal entries, June 20–25, 1757, ibid., 118.

28 Bougainville, journal entry, July 9, 1757, ibid., 124.

29 A listing of the family of Canadian settler Pierre-Louis Lorimier, who died at the western French settlement of Cap Girardeau on the banks of the Missouri in 1812, listed his wife as Charlotte Pemanpieh Bougainville, born on January 23, 1758, and by whom he had seven children. Charlotte's father is given as Louis-Antoine de Bougainville. See Cape Girardeau County Agri-Facts, http://agebb.missouri.edu/mass/agrifact/cape/narative.htm.

30 MacLeod, *The Canadian Iroquois*, 98.

31 Bougainville, journal entry, July 21, 1757, in *Adventures in the Wilderness*, 134.

32 Anderson, *Crucible of War*, 189.

33 MacLeod, *The Canadian Iroquois*, 100.

34 Anderson, *Crucible of War*, 191.

35 Bougainville, journal entry, July 24, 1757, in *Adventures in the Wilderness*, 142.

36 Ibid.

37 MacLeod, *The Canadian Iroquois*, 8.

38 Anderson, *Crucible of War*, 190.

39 Ibid., 192.

40 Bougainville, journal entry, August 9, 1757, in *Adventures in the Wilderness*, 170.

41 Ibid.

42 Anderson, *Crucible of War*, 199.

43 Bougainville, journal entries, August 15–19, 1757, in *Adventures in the Wilderness*, 174–75.

44 Ibid., 194.

45 MacLeod, *The Canadian Iroquois*, 119.

46 Bougainville, journal entry, June 26, 1757, in *Adventures in the Wilderness*, 218.

47 Ibid., 229.

48 Anderson, *Crucible of War*, 243.

49 Ibid., 246–47.

50 Bougainville, journal entries, July 14–24, 1758, in *Adventures in the Wilderness*, 246.

51 Kimbrough, *Louis-Antoine de Bougainville*, 14.

52 Ibid., 15.

53 Bougainville, journal entries, September 6–12, 1758, in *Adventures in the Wilderness*, 277.

54 Vaudreuil, to the minister, n.d., in Maurice Thiéry, *Bougainville: Soldier and Sailor* (London: Grayson and Grayson, 1932), 80.

55 Vaudreuil, to Berryer, n.d., ibid., 79.

56 Thiéry, ibid., 77.

57 Ibid.

58 Bougainville, journal entries, November 29–30, 1758, in *Adventures in the Wilderness*, 306.

59 Thiéry, *Soldier and Sailor*, 78.

60 Ibid.

CHAPTER FOUR

1   Thiéry, *Soldier and Sailor*, 81.

2   Kimbrough, *Louis-Antoine de Bougainville*, 17; also, Ross, *Bougainville*, 63.

3   Ross, *Bougainville*, 63.

4   Kimbrough, *Louis-Antoine de Bougainville*, 18.

5   Ross, *Bougainville*, 64.

6   Thiéry, *Soldier and Sailor*, 84.

7   Anderson, *Crucible of War*, 305.

8   Thiéry, *Soldier and Sailor*, 87.

9   Victor Suthren, *To Go upon Discovery: James Cook and Canada, from 1758–1779* (Toronto: Dundurn Press, 2000), 76.

10 Thiéry, *Soldier and Sailor*, 87.

11 Bougainville, journal entry, September 21, 1759, in *Adventures in the Wilderness*, 317.

12 Suthren, *To Go upon Discovery*, 79.

13 Bougainville, journal entry, September 21, 1759, in *Adventures in the Wilderness*, 318.

14 Ibid., 318–19. Actual British casualties were 433, while the French lost 70.

15 Anderson, *Crucible of War*, 349.

16 Christopher Hibbert, *Wolfe at Quebec* (Cleveland: World Publishers, 1959), 101.

17   Bougainville, journal entry, September 21, 1759, in *Adventures in the Wilderness*, 319.

18   Ross, *Bougainville*, 69.

19   Hibbert, *Wolfe at Quebec*, 132.

20   Anderson, *Crucible of War*, 352–53.

21   Ibid., 353.

22   Ross, *Bougainville*, 70.

23   Hibbert, *Wolfe at Quebec*, 133.

24   Anderson, *Crucible of War*, 355.

25   Ibid., 357.

26   Bougainville, journal entry, September 21, 1759, in *Adventures in the Wilderness*, 320.

27   Anderson, *Crucible of War*, 359–62; Hibbert, *Wolfe at Quebec*, 151–58.

28   Anderson, *Crucible of War*, 363.

29   Ross, *Bougainville*, 72.

30   Anderson, *Crucible of War*, 364.

31   Ibid., 366.

32   Ross, *Bougainville*, 75

33   Ibid., 76.

34   Ibid., 77.

35   Kimbrough, *Louis-Antoine de Bougainville*, 218 n.11.

36   Thiéry, *Soldier and Sailor*, 106.

37   Bougainville, journal *memoire* for the period since November 15, 1758, in *Adventures in the Wilderness*, 324.

38   Vaudreuil, to the minister of marine, winter 1759–60, in Ross, *Bougainville*, 74.

39   Anderson, *Crucible of War*, 388.

40   Ibid., 401.

41   Kimbrough, *Louis-Antoine de Bougainville*, 21.

42   Anderson, *Crucible of War*, 408.

43   Thiéry, *Soldier and Sailor*, 107.

CHAPTER FIVE

1   Kimbrough, *Louis-Antoine de Bougainville*, 22.

2   Thiéry, *Soldier and Sailor*, 118.

3   Bougainville, journal *memoire* for the period since November 15, 1758,

in *Adventures in the Wilderness*, 327.

4   Ibid., 328.

5   Kimbrough, *Louis-Antoine de Bougainville*, 23.

6   Ibid., 25.

7   Bougainville, journal *memoire* for the period since November 15, 1758, in *Adventures in the Wilderness*, 328.

8   Barry M. Gough, *The Falkland Islands/Malvinas: The Conquest for Empire in the South Atlantic* (London: Athlone Press, 1992), 14.

9   Kimbrough, *Louis-Antoine de Bougainville*, 33.

10   Ibid., 35.

11   Thiéry, *Soldier and Sailor*, 124.

12   Gough, *The Falkland Islands/Malvinas*, 7.

13   Ibid., 10.

14   Kimbrough, *Louis-Antoine de Bougainville*, 30.

15   Ross, *Bougainville*, 88.

16   Ibid., 89.

17   Ross, *Bougainville*, 89.

18   Kimbrough, *Louis-Antoine de Bougainville*, 40.

19   Gough, *The Falkland Islands/Malvinas*, 15–16.

20   Ibid., 16.

21   Ross, *Bougainville*, 91

22   Kimbrough, *Louis-Antoine de Bougainville*, 49.

23   Ross, *Bougainville*, 92.

24   Kimbrough, *Louis-Antoine de Bougainville*, 45.

CHAPTER SIX

1   Miriam Estensen, *Discovery: The Quest for the Great South Land* (New York: St. Martin's Press, 1999), 222.

2   Ibid., 223; Kimbrough, *Louis-Antoine de Bougainville*, 51.

3   Kimbrough, *Louis-Antoine de Bougainville*, 52.

4   John Dunmore, trans., *The Pacific Journal of Louis-Antoine de Bougainville, 1767–1768* (London: The Hakluyt Society, 2002), xlix.

5   Ibid., xliii.

6   Ibid.

7   Bougainville, journal entry, n.d., in John Dunmore, *The Pacific Journal*, xxvii.

8   Dunmore, *The Pacific Journal*, lv.

9   Kimbrough, *Louis-Antoine de Bougainville*, 55.

10   Dunmore, *The Pacific Journal*, xli.

11   Ibid., xxxix.

12   Ibid., xliv.

13   AN Colonies A 10, folio 144, Memoire from the King to M. de Bougainville; also cited in *The Pacific Journal*, xlv.

14   AN B2 382, folios 85, 492, minister to Bougainville; cited in *The Pacific Journal*, xlviii.

15   Kimbrough, *Louis-Antoine de Bougainville*, 61.

16   Bougainville, journal entry, n.d., cited in Kimbrough, *Louis-Antoine de Bougainville*, 62.

17   Dunmore, *The Pacific Journal*, li.

18   Thiéry, *Soldier and Sailor*, 159.

19   Ibid., 160.

20   Ibid., 162.

21   Ibid., 170.

22   Kimbrough, *Louis-Antoine de Bougainville*, 73.

23   Ross, *Bougainville*, 105.

24   Bougainville, journal entry, December 4–5, 1767, in *The Pacific Journal*, 7.

25   Bougainville, journal entry, December 7–8, 1767, ibid., 10.

26   Ibid.

27   Ibid., 11.

28   Ibid.

29   Ibid., 10n.

30   Ross, *Bougainville*, 111.

31   Bougainville, journal entry, January 16, 1768, in *The Pacific Journal*, 31.

32   Bougainville, journal entry, January 6, 1768, ibid., 27.

33   Ibid., 32.

34   Ibid., 33.

35   Ibid., 34.

36   Ibid., 36.

37   Bougainville, journal entries, February 18–20, 1768, ibid., 41.

38   Ibid., 48.

39   Ross, *Bougainville*, 114.

40   Bougainville, journal entry, April 1–2, 1768, in *The Pacific Journal*, 55.

41   Ibid., 59.

42   Bougainville, journal entry, April 15, 1768, ibid., 76.

43   Bougainville, journal entry, May 23, 1768, ibid., 93.

44   Bougainville, journal entry, June 6, 1768, ibid., 100.

45   Bougainville, journal entry, July 29, 1768, ibid., 112.

46   Bougainville, journal entry, August 25, 1768, ibid., 126.

47   Kimbrough, *Louis-Antoine de Bougainville*, 116.

48   Ibid., 119.

Chapter Seven

1   George Robertson, cited in Frank Sherry, *Pacific Passions: The European Struggle for Power in the Great Ocean in the Age of Exploration* (New York: Morrow, 1994), 310.

2   Bougainville, journal entry, n.d., in Dunmore, *The Pacific Journal*, 60.

3   Ibid., 61.

4   Ibid., 62.

5   Ibid., 63.

6   Ibid.

7   Hammond, *News from New Cythera*, 23–27 *passim*.

8   Commerson, in Ross, *Bougainville*, 120–11.

9   Alan Moorehead, *The Fatal Impact: An Account of the Invasion of the South Pacific, 1767–1840* (London: The Reprint Society, 1966), 46.

10   Dunmore, *The Pacific Journal*, lviii.

11   William Wales, "Remarks on Mr. Forster's Account of Captain Cook's Last Voyage, 1778," in *Exploration and Exchange: A South Seas Anthology, 1680–1900*, ed. Jonathan Lamb, Vanessa Smith, and Nicholas Thomas (Chicago: U. of Chicago Press, 2000), 104.

12   Bernard Smith, *European Vision and the South Pacific* (New Haven: Yale University Press, 1985), 148–49.

Chapter Eight

1   Kimbrough, *Louis-Antoine de Bougainville*, 126.

2   Ibid., 129.

3   Ibid.

4   Ibid., 132.

5   Ross, *Bougainville*, 149.

6   Ibid.

7   Kimbrough, *Louis-Antoine de Bougainville*, 129.

8   Ibid., 138.

9   Ibid., 141.

10 Ross, *Bougainville*, 152.

11 Ibid., 153.

12 Ibid.

13 Kimbrough, *Louis-Antoine de Bougainville*, 148.

14 Ibid., 158.

15 Ibid., 168.

16 Ibid., 170.

17 Colonel H. L. Landers, "The Sea Battle off the Capes of Virginia," from "The Viriginia Campaign and the Blockade and Siege of Yorktown, 1781," United States Army Center for Military History, http://www.army.mil/CMH-pg/books/RevWar/Yorktown/AWC-Ytn-fm.htm.

18 Joseph B. Mitchell, *Decisive Battles of the American Revolution* (Greenwich, Conn.: Fawcett, 1964), 213.

19 Ross, *Bougainville*, 157.

20 Kimbrough, *Louis-Antoine de Bougainville*, 190.

CHAPTER NINE

1   Ross, *Bougainville*, 160.

2   Ibid., 162.

3   Kimbrough, *Louis-Antoine de Bougainville*, 183.

4   Richard Walter, *A Voyage Round the World in the Years 1740–44* (Geneva: n.p., 1885), 120.

Select Bibliography

Primary Sources

Papers relating to Louis-Antoine de Bougainville are located in the *Archives Nationaux*, Paris, under the number AN 155 AP 1-4. Papers relating to the Malouines settlement may be found in AN Colonies F2 A20; AN Marine C1 175, 178, and 180 contain French naval officers' service records, including those of Bougainville. Kimbrough (1990) makes extensive use of these papers in her fine biography.

The lay student may be aided by recent and previous publications of Bougainville's most significant journals, notably Edward Hamilton's translation of Bougainville's American Journals (University of Oklahoma Press, 1964) and John Dunmore's meticulous presentation of the Journal of Bougainville's Pacific voyage (The Hakluyt Society, 2002).

Secondary Sources

Anderson, Fred. *Crucible of War.* New York: Knopf, 2000.

Barratt, Glynn. *The Tuamotu Islands and Tahiti.* Vancouver: UBC Press, 1992.

Beaglehole, J.C. *The Exploration of the Pacific.* 3rd ed. Stanford, Calif.: Stanford University Press, 1966.

Boissel, Thierry. *Bougainville, ou, l'homme de l'unive.* Paris: Orban, 1991.

Bougainville, Louis-Antoine de. *Adventures in the Wilderness: The American Journals of Louis-Antoine de Bougainville, 1756–1760.* Translated and edited by Edward Hamilton. Norman, Okla.: University of Oklahoma Press, 1964.

———. *A Voyage Round the World.* Translated by John Reinhold Forster. London: J. Nourse, 1772.

Dunmore, John, trans. and ed. *The Pacific Journal of Louis-Antoine de Bougainville, 1767–1768.* London: The Hakluyt Society, 2002.

Edwards, Philip, ed. *The Journals of Captain Cook.* London: Penguin, 1999.

Estensen, Miriam. *Discovery: The Quest for the Great South Land.* New York: St. Martin's Press, 1999.

Forster, Johann Reinhold. *Observations Made during a Voyage Round the World.* Nicholas Thomas, Harriet Guest, and Michael Dettelbach, eds. Honolulu: U. of Hawaii Press, 1996.

Gough, Barry M.. *The Falkland Islands/Malvinas: The Contest for Empire in the South Pacific.* London: Athlone Press, 1992.

Hammond, Lincoln Davis, ed. *News from New Cythera: A Report of Bougainville's Voyage, 1766–1769.* Minneapolis: U. of Minnesota Press, 1970.

Hibbert, Christopher. *Wolfe at Quebec.* Cleveland: World Publishers, 1959.

Irwin, Geoffrey. *The Prehistoric Exploration and Colonisation of the Pacific.* Cambridge: Cambridge University Press, 1992.

Kerallain, René de. *La jeunesse de Bougainville et la guerre de sept ans.* Paris: Daupeley-Gouverneur, 1896.

Kimbrough, Mary. *Louis-Antoine de Bougainville, 1729–1811.* Lewiston, N.Y.: E. Mellen Press, 1990.

Lamb, Jonathan, Vanessa Smith, and Nicholas Thomas, eds. *Exploration and Exchange: A South Seas Anthology, 1680–1900.* Chicago: U. of Chicago Press, 2000.

MacLeod, D. Peter. *The Canadian Iroquois and the Seven Years' War.* Toronto: Dundurn Press, 1996.

Mahan, A.T. *The Influence of Sea Power upon History.* Boston: Little, Brown, 1895.

Manceron, Claude. *The Twilight of the Old Order, 1774–1778.* New York: Alfred A. Knopf, 1977.

Martin-Allanic, Jean-Étienne. *Bougainville, navigateur et les decouvertes de son temps.* 2 vols. Paris: Presses universitaires de France, 1964.

Mitchell, Joseph B. *Decisive Battles of the American Revolution.* Greenwich, Conn.: Fawcett, 1964.

Moorehead, Alan. *The Fatal Impact: An Account of the Invasion of the South Pacific, 1767–1840.* London: The Reprint Society, 1966.

Ogg, David. *Europe of the Ancien Régime, 1715–1783.* New York: Harper & Row, 1965.

Owen, John B. *The Eighteenth Century, 1714–1815.* New York: Norton, 1974.

Parkman, Francis. *A Half-Century of Conflict.* New York: Collier, 1962.

———. *France and England in North America.* New York: F. Ungar, 1965.

Ross, Michael. *Bougainville.* London: Gordon and Cremonesi, 1978.

Selby, John. *The Road to Yorktown.* New York: St. Martin's Press, 1976.

Sherry, Frank. *Pacific Passions: The European Struggle for Power in the Great Ocean in the Age of Exploration.* New York: Morrow, 1994.

Smith, B.: *European Vision and the South Pacific.* New Haven: Yale University Press, 2nd edition, 1984.

Spate, O.H.K.: *Paradise Found and Lost.* Toronto: Pergamon Press Canada, 1988.

Suthren, Victor. *To Go upon Discovery: James Cook and Canada, from 1758 to 1779.* Toronto: Dundurn Press, 2000.

Taillemite, Étienne. "Louis-Antoine de Bougainville," from *Dictionary of Canadian Biography.* Toronto: University of Toronto Press, n.d., 5:102–105.

Thiéry, Maurice. *Bougainville, Soldier and Sailor.* London: Grayson & Grayson, 1932.

Van Loon, Hendrik Willem. *The Story of the Pacific.* New York: Harcourt, Brace, 1940.